HOW TO L

PAYING AIRLINE JOB

The PROVEN System for Beating the Odds and Landing Pilot Jobs at the World's Best Airlines

Rick Hogan

Published by V1 consulting

Anchorage, AK

Unattributed quotations attributed to Rick Hogan.

Second Edition

Library of Congress Cataloguing-in Publication Data has been applied for

ISBN-13:
978-1495233609

ISBN-10:
149523360X

Introduction

've been asked more than once how this book came to be, considering the fact that I am by trade a pilot, and not a writer. The simple answer is this: sometimes in life you find yourself in a situation you never anticipated, and something unexpected comes along as a result. This book is the unexpected result of not only applying and interviewing more than I ever anticipated in my career, but of pondering those two processes often. Too often, some would say. In the unpredictable worldwide airline industry, you play the cards you're dealt. The funny thing is it's not just the cards that are unpredictable, but the whole game.

I read a lot of books about how to be successful at getting jobs. Pilot jobs specifically. I would go so far as to say I have probably read everything that's on the market with regard to how to ace your interview and get a good airline job. After reading each book, I had the feeling I'd just been the recipient of a very "academic" lecture. Not once did I have the impression that the person doing the writing had been sitting where I was. I read some books that covered so much technical information there was no possible way (for me, anyway) to retain it all.

It was like the author was saying, "Here's all you need to know for your interview: Everything."

How is this book any different from the ones that have been on the market for, literally, decades? Is it the snappier cover? Are there bigger words? Is there more excruciatingly obscure technical information? This book is different not because of those things, specifically, but because someone who's sat exactly where you are right now wrote it; someone who needed to know what works and what doesn't in an airline interview, and who had a whole career riding on it.

And it's written by someone who has been successful at what would be considered by almost anyone as some of the most demanding and competitive interviews in the world.

What was I looking for in those other books that I couldn't find? Something more than just regurgitated facts and technical trivia. I didn't really care about how to calculate the groundspeed at which a tire will hydroplane (unless they were going to ask me that specifically, of course). I cared about what the interviewers wanted to see, and how to show it to them.

A long time ago in a galaxy far away, a pivotal opportunity dropped unexpectedly in my lap. I was asked if I wanted to come to the corporate office after a trip I was flying and interview some pilot applicants.

I thought, "What better way to learn about how to interview than by sitting on the other side of the table for a while?"

I'd like to say I became an interviewer for the good of the company (and maybe even the world!), but it was more selfish than that. I wanted to learn how to interview well myself by watching others. Believe me when I say that, after working in the recruiting department at a regional airline for years, I saw both sides of the spectrum. Both *extreme* sides. From applicants you felt like you would be lucky to get, to the ones you considered calling security to get them out of the building. I interviewed them all.

Despite interviewing literally hundreds of pilots in that time, when *my* first major airline interview came up I felt unprepared and, frankly, a little panicked. After all, this was the shot I'd been working my entire career to get, and failure wasn't an option.

I acquired the few airline interview books I didn't already own and scoured them, looking for any insight to ensure I capitalized on my opportunity. Spending a lot of money and time reading these books, I never found one that really spoke to me from the pilot's perspective. That frustrated me...and this book is the result. Here you will find the culmination of my experiences hiring (or not hiring) pilots, and being interviewed myself at some of the top airlines in the world. From one pilot to another.

Airline interviews are like getting struck by lightning. They happen infrequently, sometimes unexpectedly, and rarely in the same place twice. Airline interviews are also a little like lottery tickets. Thousands and thousands of people pay to play, but not everyone wins. When you are the person holding that potential winning ticket, you need to make sure you can cash it in.

This book can teach you effective ways to create and take advantage of an interview opportunity. Many pilots get interviews, but not all of them get the job. When your opportunity comes around, you want to be the person cashing in that lottery ticket, not the one sitting around dreaming of "what might have been."

After being in this situation a number of times, my preparation method became a systematic exercise. It worked each time. Instead of walking into an interview and *hoping* for a good outcome, I walked in knowing I was as prepared as humanly possible. This systematic method worked for every airline, whether it was a regional, US Legacy, world-class foreign carrier, cargo, package delivery... you name it.

I don't want to bore you with superfluous junk and arbitrarily tell you "my story." I've done that in enough interviews to last a lifetime. If you're going to invest your time and effort in this method, however, you need a little of the history to have confidence in it.

As a much better writer than myself once said, "I want you to have all the background."

So, Rick, tell us a little about yourself...

Some years ago, I got called for an interview with a US Legacy passenger carrier. The company was at the top of my list of career destinations. I had the proverbial lottery ticket in my hand. In my mind, I was already bidding 747-400 Captain and inventorying all the houses, boats, planes, and ex-wives I'd be acquiring (just kidding about the ex-wives, honey). The interview just seemed like a formality to what I thought was surely my destiny.

In addition to reading the airline interview books I was obsessively acquiring, I contacted a lady (let's call her Jane Doe) who specialized in interview preparation for this particular company. I spent some more money on a two-hour telephone prep, and at the end she said I was good to go. Now I was surely unstoppable. After all, Jane knew all the questions they would ask and she told me what they wanted to hear. What could go wrong?

This is what! The first question they asked me when I walked into the interview, *the absolute first*, was, "Have you done interview preparation with Jane Doe?"

One important rule to live by is *never lie in an interview.* I had the immediate impression they didn't view this prep as a good thing, but I took my own advice and admitted I had. To make a long story short, they didn't ask me one single question this lady had gone over in the interview prep. Not one! Not even a variation of one.

The interview prep I did with Jane Doe took about two hours. If that prep were all I'd done to prepare for the interview, I would have tanked without any doubt. Luckily, I spent the remainder of the two weeks leading up to this interview refining and implementing my own system of preparation. Unlike Jane Doe's, my system didn't require me to know the questions. The method I developed prepared me for *any* question, and it worked.

I have used this system over and over again. I've interviewed with cargo companies, foreign carriers, package delivery companies, training departments…you name it. This system has never let me down. People around me started noticing I was having more luck getting interviews and jobs than the average Joe. Many of my peers were still "building time" while I got checked out in the 747-400 and had multiple job offers, all while the economy was down. Everyone wanted to know what I was doing differently. I taught many pilots my very methodical system for application and preparation. It worked for them. This system has worked for pilots at nearly every major airline in the US and numerous companies worldwide. It has been tried and proven.

Relying on someone else to provide you with all the questions and answers you need puts an incredible amount of faith in them, especially when you've got a major career milestone riding on it. The method I use teaches you how to open your own doors and show your interviewers what they want to see, without needing someone to lead you by the hand. No one has more riding on the successful outcome of your interview than you do. At the end of the day, the interview prep guy or gal has some limited interest in your success, because they all want their clients to do well. The opportunity that gets lost, however, is yours and yours alone. It may be a job opportunity you won't get another chance at.

That's why I developed this system and put it down on paper (or e-paper I guess, as the case may be). You don't want to depend on anyone but yourself for your success. This method will give you the tools you need to be successful in *any* interview. You don't need to know all the questions beforehand. All you need to know is what your interviewers are looking for and how to show it to them.

I've made mistakes along the way, to be sure. I've also seen an awful lot of interview mistakes happen. If you're taking the time to read this book, I'm going to guess you've been flying airplanes for a little while. You know by now that nothing makes you learn faster than a gigantic am-I-really-still-alive mistake.

Have you ever set the parking brake and uttered the words, "Wow, I'll never do that again"?

You learned from a mistake, and probably became a better pilot because of it.

Mistakes are great potential learning experiences, but they can be expensive on many different levels. Learning from your own mistakes in an interview can cost you a job you may need, affect your confidence, and totally alter your career path. You're going to learn from others' interview mistakes now, so you don't do the same when it counts.

In this book, I've included a lot of examples of people who learned the hard way, by making big mistakes in their own interviews. My intention is *not* to make fun of them. I'm *not* saying they're bad people, or even bad pilots. If I approach a situation from a tongue-in-cheek perspective, it's because that's how I approach life in general. I'm not trying to judge or be disrespectful to anyone whose actions have found their way onto these pages.

There, but for the grace of God, go I. That's an incredibly important phrase to remember in aviation. It applies to interviews in aviation as well.

As you read through these examples of what not to do (which I've accurately titled *Interview Train Wrecks*), learn the hard lessons from these individuals' mistakes and you won't be forced to learn from your own.

Strolling into any situation without a plan is a recipe for disaster. Whether it's flying, interviewing, or simply crossing the street. The odds you'll screw up are high if you haven't done any forethought. Being successful means having a plan and putting it into action.

I have an interview train wreck story of my own, which I'll give you the specifics on later. It happened early in my career, long before I had a solid method of preparation in place and because I had *no* plan whatsoever. As I sauntered in on interview day, I thought I'd "wing it." I overestimated my conversational skills, technical knowledge, and general sharpness. The results were a foregone conclusion; I just didn't realize it until it was too late. I have looked like a tremendous fool on a few specific occasions in my life. This was definitely one of them. Walking into an interview cold is like blindly throwing a dart at a board and hoping it's a bull's eye. Without serious preparation on your part, success can be a million to one shot.

At the end of each section, I've provided a summary of the key points you want to take away from it. The points themselves are merely reminders; the explanation of how to use each concept to your full advantage is contained in this book. I'm going to warn you right now, this isn't *The Quick and Easy Guide to Scam Your Interviewers and Fool Them into Hiring You*. Being truly prepared and succeeding takes time and effort, but it will be time and effort well spent when you walk through the door on interview day. Like everything in life, you will only get out of it what you put into it.

Part 1

Create opportunity

Opening the doors

Aviation experts, flight schools, and nearly everyone else who makes a profit from your training have been predicting pilot shortages since...well...probably since forever. The "looming" shortage is predicted and re-predicted, caused by a combination of massive retirements, airline expansion, and exponentially increasing air travel demand. Companies will be on the verge of shutting down because they can't find enough pilots to crew their aircraft. Time to captain upgrade will be practically nothing. The hiring doors will swing wide open at every airline in the country, and indeed the world. You, as someone who has wisely decided to capitalize on this almost certain shortage, will simply sit back and decide where you'd like to spend your career.

I first heard this exciting tale when I was working on my private pilot certificate at a major aviation university. I heard about the "coming" pilot shortage, and it sounded plausible. Even better, it sounded easy. All I had to do was sit back, relax, and wait for the industry to come to me.

Unfortunately, the pilot shortage I envision seems to always be just over the horizon, riding a unicorn to the other end of the rainbow. I keep waiting for recruiters from major airlines around the world to come

1

knocking on my door, trying to outbid each other for my services. It keeps *not* happening, but hey, here's to hoping.

The reality is this: there are actually cyclical periods when a lot of hiring takes place. A more accurate term than "pilot shortage" is "hiring cycle." Here's an important thing to keep in mind: just because you may be lucky enough to find yourself in the middle of a great hiring cycle does not guarantee you a top-paying job in the airline industry. An "open door hiring" mentality at top tier companies is what those of us in the real world refer to as a pipe dream. There will never be an open door policy at leading companies. They *always* have more applicants than positions, and for this reason they can be as picky as they want with whom they hire.

Don't jump off a bridge just yet. That doesn't mean there won't be plenty of opportunities. There will be times when significant hiring is happening at all levels of the industry, from bottom-rung-time-builder-jobs all the way up to the career destination airlines. But mark my words: there will *always* be a high level of competition for the top spots. Always! The better the company, the higher the competition will be.

There's nothing wrong with flying 12 legs a day in a Beech 1900. If you're happy with that particular gig for a career (and there are some who are), more power to you. For many, however, there will come a time when handling the passengers, loading the bags, and not having a bathroom get pretty old. It actually gets a little old the first time you're forced to keep an empty water bottle next to your seat, "just in case." Thus many pilots at this level look to move up the ladder. Everyone likes better quality of life, more comfortable equipment, better pay, and the natural progression up Maslow's hierarchy of needs. You may spend some time in that 1900, and then decide it's time to enter the interview fray once more.

In good times, when the industry is moving steadily, you'll be competing with hundreds of similarly qualified pilots. If the industry is stagnant, which it cyclically is, you'll literally be competing with thousands of similarly qualified pilots for available jobs. You need to find ways to stand out from the pack and get noticed before your peers. Let's start there.

Online applications

So, the two million dollar question is: what trips the trigger to get the interview call? Here's the evasive answer: only the people sorting the applicants actually know, and they're generally tight lipped on what they're looking for at any given time. And it changes. Case in point: a major package delivery company was hiring directly into wide-body aircraft for a base with almost exclusively international operations. They decided they wanted to interview mainly candidates with previous heavy-jet international experience. If you, as an applicant, fell into that experience window and had exactly what they were looking for at that time, you got called before people who had more flight time than you, more recommendation letters than you, were better looking than you, etc.

In the old days, if you knew the right person, your application could quickly find its way to the top of the stack. The time it took to get an interview was directly related to how well regarded your contact(s) were by the people running the interview show. If you were a good networker, this made things easy. However, if you didn't know a soul at the company you were trying to get a job at, you were last in line behind all the other people who did.

For better or worse, most of the big companies have moved away from this model with computerized application systems. There are still companies that operate under the "wink-wink-nod-nod" recommendation method, but they are getting fewer and further between. What that means to you, with regard to top tier companies, is that a significant portion of the human element has been removed from the equation. Your buddy from flight school can't go have coffee with the chief pilot and all of a sudden you've got an interview scheduled.

4

Now, it's all about the data. You enter all your pertinent information in an online application which asks for all kinds of strange breakdowns of your flight time i.e., how many night simulated instrument landings from NDB approaches do you have? Once you get the whole thing filled out, you become a resident of the airlines' applicant database. Congratulations.

Now, in the old days, we would group resumes and paper applications together based on flight time, qualifications, and internal recommendations. An actual real-live person reviewed each and every application package. Today, your application gets pulled from the database based on what the company is looking for at any given time. Think of the computer based process as a big point-based system. This is a little bit of an oversimplification, but it works for understanding the basis of how most database-driven application systems work. If the company puts a lot of value on having previous airline experience, you get a point for that. If it puts value on having jet pilot in command (PIC) experience, you get a point for that. Then, maybe another point if you have 5000 hours or more of said PIC. Check airman? IOE instructor? Give yourself another point. Have a letter of recommendation on file? Maybe you get 2 points for that, depending on how important it is to the company. Get the idea?

Now you can probably see where this is going. All applicants get ranked based on their score. When the company is ready to interview, they pull the top 100 names and call them in. Once that round of interviews is complete, the next 100 get called, etc. Interspersed in there can be an element of chance, where a certain percentage of applicants get called at random and aren't necessarily at the top of the point-based list.

We'll talk specifically about how to be competitive in this particular environment shortly, but for now let's stick with general online application stuff. Two of the most frequent errors applicants make with online applications are:

1. Missing data fields that you should fill in
2. Filling in incorrect information

It's easy to miss a checkbox that says, "Check here if you've never had an accident, incident, or violation." Think you get a point for checking that box? Probably. Also, make sure to read the text associated with each data field carefully. I've read some really poorly worded statements that left me thinking, "Wait, am I supposed to check this box or not?"

Don't leave data fields blank if they apply to you. For example, if the application asks when you stopped working for your current employer, and you're still working there, put "not applicable" or "N/A." Leaving fields blank can raise a question of whether you meant to do that or just missed it. If you put N/A, it shows you did actually look at it, but that specific field doesn't apply to you.

No matter how automated and computer-based these systems get, you still need to take some time and proofread your work. Spellchecker won't catch the fact you put 500 instead of 5000 in your multi-engine jet column, and that will affect your ranking. That may seem like a ridiculous mistake, but when you're filling in literally hundreds of data fields it's easy to drop a zero here or there. Do yourself a favor once the whole thing is completed: take a break for a while, and then come back to the application. Check through *every single* piece of information you've entered. Don't de-rail your application before it even gets started by being sloppy with the information you're putting in.

Creating the right résumé

Curriculum vitae (CV), résumé: are these things still relevant in our digital world? Believe it or not, a good résumé never goes out of style, and if you take some time to create an effective one, you'll find yourself using it more than you think.

There's the question then, what makes a résumé effective? The trashcans of airline hiring departments all over the world are filled with crappy résumés. I don't mean crappy in that the owners of those résumés aren't qualified. I mean crappy in that they look like they were put together by a 5th grader with ADHD (which would actually be kind of insulting to the 5th grader now that I think about it).

What do you want a good résumé to do? Should it look pretty, like a piece of art? Should it contain your life story? Negative, on all counts. A résumé should be a clear, concise document that a reviewer can *quickly* scan to get an idea of your qualifications, work history, and education. That's it. Reviewers spend no more than *approximately 6 seconds* scanning your résumé. They don't want to spend any more time than that. If they have to, it will instantly annoy them. Knowing that now, your résumé must be effectively formatted to show them everything they need to see in that 6-second window.

Some of the weirder pilot résumés I've seen contain: pictures of the applicant on the front page (and not just a head and shoulders shot; I saw one where a guy included a series of photos of himself from what looked like a modeling photo shoot. Weird), strange colored paper (blue stands out in my mind), multiple pages stapled together, and strange ink colors that are not black, just to name a few.

You don't need or want a résumé that stands out because the format is "different" or "unique." You want your résumé to stand out because of your qualifications and experience. Think of your résumé, as you should all the documentation you submit both paper and electronic, as an extension of yourself. You want your résumé to be clear, concise, and easy to read. It should be one page, *and one page only.* The résumé's purpose is to provide a quick rundown of your qualifications and experience, nothing more. It should not be a narrative that tells your life story; that is what the interview is for. I won't say never, but you will *almost never* get hired just by submitting a résumé. The résumé's only purpose is to list your qualifications so you can be further evaluated in an interview.

The first line item on your résumé should be the objective. With it you're stating the position for which you're applying. Include the name of the company you're applying to on this line. That way it doesn't seem so much like you just printed out 100 résumés and blasted them everywhere.

The flight times can be modified to include whatever categories you need for the job. For example, you don't need to include floatplane time unless it's a floatplane job you're applying for. Whatever the minimum flight time requirements and categories are for a particular job, make sure to include them in your flight time summary. That way an employer can see at a quick glance that you meet the minimum qualifications to apply.

The next and most important section is "Experience." This is where you set yourself apart from the other applicants. "Experience" is where you detail everything you've done and everything you can bring to a new employer. Summarize every additional job, project, or department you've been able to be a part of. Make sure you mention experiences a potential pilot employer would find interesting. The fact that you were the captain of your intramural Frisbee golf team is great, but it's not pertinent to your pilot résumé. Only include items that have some kind of professional significance. Working at Starbucks isn't applicable, unless you were the manager. If you developed a safety program for Starbucks, that would be something worth including.   If you're low on aviation-specific experience, focus on jobs that require leadership and initiative.

The last section is your educational experience, and it's pretty self-explanatory.   If you're fresh out of school, your educational background is all you have to demonstrate what kind of an employee you'll potentially be. Eventually, as you gain it, your work experience will take precedence over your educational background.   Until then, it may be all you've got.   If you're proud of your GPA, it's worth including. Honors and achievements can be included, especially if you're short on aviation-specific experience.   You can also list academic positions of leadership and initiative.   Just make sure to keep the total résumé to one page.

A solid résumé is like a good handshake.   You don't want someone to remember it because it was formatted differently from the norm.   If you effectively build your résumé using the techniques we're going to cover, your résumé will stand out for the right reasons.

The following résumé format has been very effective for me personally. I recommend it to anyone and everyone. It's a very concise, easy to read presentation giving employers all the information they need and nothing they don't:

John William Doe

1522 Seclusion Cove Drive
Anniston, NY 12515
Cell (123) 456-7890   Home (123) 456-7890
Email: JWDoe@massmail.com

OBJECTIVE: To obtain a flight officer position

LICENSES:
Airline Transport Pilot Certificate
B757, B767, MD-11 type ratings
Commercial Privileges: Airplane Single Engine Land
Medical Certificate: FAA Class I

FLIGHT TIME: **TOTAL 7047**

Pilot in Command	3225	Jet	4710
Second in Command	3522	Jet PIC	1713
Turbine PIC	2724	Turboprop	1771

EXPERIENCE: **INSTRUCTOR PILOT**

01/08 - Present   ABC Airlines   Train and evaluate 757/767 flight crews. Perform
New York, NY   worldwide line pilot operations on 757/767.

AIRLINE PILOT

06/05 – 01/08   XYZ Airlines   Captain and First Officer on B747-400
Chicago, IL   performing worldwide cargo and passenger
operations.

AIRLINE PILOT

07/04 – 05/05   Cargo Carrier   First Officer on 757/767 performing domestic
Los Angeles, CA   passenger operations.

CRM FACILITATOR

07/00 – 11/03   Regional Airline   Instructed CRM ground school. Assisted in the
Atlanta, GA   development of CRM course and training aids.

AIRLINE PILOT

03/98 – 07/04   Regional Airline   Captain on CR2 and B1900. First Officer on the CR2
Atlanta, GA   and EMB-120.

EDUCATION: **BACHELOR OF SCIENCE DEGREE**

08/93 – 12/97   Parks College Aeronautical University   Bachelor of Science in Aeronautical Science
St. Louis, MO   Area of Concentration: Airline Pilot
Graduated Cum Laude CGPA 3.64/4.0

10

Dress up your contact information

Before you send your résumé out or start shot-gunning applications all over the industry, always, always, always check your contact information. As a pilot, you're basically one step away from being a modern-day nomad. Make sure all the phone numbers, physical addresses, and email addresses you list *can actually* be used to contact you. I know some folks who have missed great opportunities because they listed a phone number they only check once every few weeks. Imagine their surprise when there's a two-week-old message asking them to come in for an interview. Now, imagine their disappointment when they respond to said message and find there aren't any more interview slots available.

While you're making sure all your contact information is up to date, also make sure the information you're using is suitable. You may have been using assman6969@mail.com as your email address for years, and while I understand that you love it, it might be time to come up with something a little more professional. Your friends can still use your "hilarious" assman address. You don't have to get rid of it, just come up with something that looks a little better on your résumé, unless your name is really Assman. In that case, my condolences.

Another thing you'll want to update is your voicemail. I remember leaving some messages (or deciding not to) to voicemail greetings such as:

"Hey, it's Mike. If I'm not answering, it's because I'm HAMMERED!"

or

"Yo, this is Joe. When you hear the beep, let it go."

Joe's is verbatim. I actually wrote it down because it made me laugh. Keep in mind: an "amusing" voicemail greeting may not have that intended effect. While it may seem clever right now, many recruiters and human resource representatives have had their sense of humor surgically removed. Make sure your voicemail message is something friendly, yet professional and conservative. Imagine something you would hear when calling your local bank. I know that's not as entertaining as a voicemail message that screams obscenities at your listener, but you can change it back once you get the job.

Points to remember

- ✓ Your résumé should be clear, concise, and limited to one page.
- ✓ Build a better résumé through experience and it will get noticed. Break down special projects and duties under the "Experience" section.
- ✓ Check your résumé contact information and make sure it's current.
- ✓ Have professional voicemail and email addresses in place.

Your logbooks are you on paper

Your logbooks are a physical representation of you and how professionally you conduct yourself in your chosen trade as an airline pilot. Sometimes, the first impression you make with your interviewers is with your logbooks, other times they'll be looked at while you're being interviewed. The quality of your logbooks will *absolutely* make an impression. Make sure it's a good one.

Interview Train Wreck #1

While the applicants were taking their written tests on interview day, an intern would collect their logbooks. We would use that test time to review the logbooks prior to the interview. On this particular day, the intern came in with the stack of standard Jeppesen-style logbooks, and one notable exception: a pile of 5 paper day planners forming a little pyramid at the top. By day planners, I mean small paper calendar books about the size of a checkbook. I was curious what they were all about, so I was the first to grab them.

The day planners had the numbers 1-5 written on the front in black marker. I opened numero uno and saw the applicant had been recording his flight time on the calendar along with notes about what he had planned for that day.

For example: "Buy milk, bread, eggs, case of Coke. Flew 1.2." or "Dinner with Suzie @ 6. Flew 1.5."

At the bottom of each page was a circled number. I found that, after adding up each individual entry, this number was the total flight time for the month. Awesome. Definitely lacking some professionalism, but it still does the job, I guess. Maybe his logbooks were burned up in a fire and this was his backup or something. I always try to give everyone the benefit of the doubt.

In the interview, after the initial pleasantries I asked, "I've never seen logbooks kept quite like yours. Why do you prefer the day planners to a more traditional style?"

It seemed like he was ready for this question. I guessed this issue came up for him on another occasion, because he snapped back with no hesitation, "There's no law that says how I have to keep a record of my flight time. I can do it any way I want."

The red flags were waving in the wind now.

"I agree," I said. "I'm just asking why you prefer a day planner to a specifically formatted logbook?"

"It's easy," he replied, sounding incredulous. Apparently he thought it was a stupid question.

"Oh, I see," I responded. "I didn't realize it was easy. Thanks."

What was easy was my decision not to recommend him.

It doesn't matter where you interview, your logbooks are going to be reviewed. I've had interviews where they've been casually flipped through, and the other extreme where someone literally poured over them entry by entry with a fine-tooth comb. When you're talking about logbooks, it's best to prepare for the worst and hope for the best.

The guy in the Interview Train Wreck above was absolutely correct. You can keep records of your flight time any way you want. You can write it down on used bar napkins or engrave it into stone tablets. However you do it, keep in mind that someday, someone will be looking through said bar napkins deciding whether or not to give you a job. Since you are interviewing for a position where there is an expectation of a high level of professionalism, accuracy, and attention to detail, you want that to be reflected in your logbook. Plan accordingly.

Almost everyone's primary training logbooks are a mess, mine included. During your very first student cross-country, you don't consider that someday, years down the road, an anal-retentive paperwork-Nazi is going to be scrutinizing every entry you've ever made. My very first logbook has scratch outs. It had comments like, "Made Mike puke" and "Bitchin x-wind!" and it had mathematical errors. Over time, it slowly dawned on me that an interviewer who saw those things might not view me as the professional aviator I really was. The one that was deep, deep, deep down inside. So, I took some whiteout and tried to dress it up a little. It didn't look great, but it was much better than the alternative.

When my training was complete, I closed that logbook out and started a new one. This one was going to be my "professional" logbook. It was big and brown and had my name written on the front in gold. Nothing says professional like having your name written in *gold*. I kept my daily flights in a small trip log I carried with me. Every so often I transferred all the trip log entries into the master logbook, which got tedious. Pretty soon, I was just transferring the total for the day. Before long it was just the total for the month, and I rationalized it because it was…easy.

I got called for an interview after using that method for a while, and I went back through my logbook to review it. You could clearly see my enthusiasm wane over the course of the pages as the entries went from one entry each flight, then one entry each day, and finally to one entry each month.

I imagined my answer in an interview if they asked why the manner in which I kept my records changed over time.

"Because it's easy. Duh."

I heard myself say it in the exact same voice day-planner guy had said it to me years before. I decided right then my logbooks needed a total reboot. I went online *that night* and downloaded electronic logbook software. Then began the long and painful process of

15

transferring all my flight time into it, leg by leg, and then printing it out, page by page. It was a full-time job in and of itself. When I was done (nearly two weeks later) I felt like I'd really accomplished something. My logbook finally looked as professional as it needed to, and I felt confident handing it over to anyone.

Your logbooks are a part of you. When they are laid out in front of an interviewer on the table, they're examining you, not just looking through your records. Professionalism, accuracy, and attention to detail are all immediately conveyed through a set of well-kept logbooks. I've seen logbooks that were homemade excel spreadsheets, dot-matrix printouts, day planners, and everything in between.

I've even had a guy hand me his laptop and say, "It's all in here."

I'm sure it was all in there. That doesn't mean I want to sift through all the donkey-porn on his computer in order to find it. Don't force your interviewers to interpret the unconventional system you've come up with for keeping your flight time. There's no need to show them how creative you are by designing your own logbook. Keep a standard Jeppesen-style logbook. Electronic logbooks will print hard copies in this format as well. No one will *ever* have any issues with that. Keeping flight records leg by leg is a pain (I know from experience), but no one can *ever* argue with that method. If they do, they're just trying to push your buttons, which can happen.

There are numerous electronic logbooks that work great and take a lot of pain out of record keeping. In fact, it's so simple now there's really no excuse not to do it the right way. You can keep your daily records in a smart phone, then sync it to your main logbook when you have time. Print the pages out in the Jeppesen-style format and bind them in a professional looking cover. Electronic logbooks do the math for you, are always neat and legible, and present very well. I recommend an electronic solution as opposed to the old-school handwritten log, but either one will work.

One technique I always use, regardless of the type of logbook, is to total all my flight times in pencil on the last page. The entries on the last page of your logbook will usually stop somewhere in the middle of the sheet. That flight time will not be totaled, since you haven't completed the entries for that page (some e-logbooks may do this for you; mine doesn't). Your interviewers want your total times, right up to the day of your interview. They will have to add up the remaining entries on the partially completed page if you haven't already. I always total that last page in pencil, so an interviewer can look at the bottom of your last page and immediately see how much flight time you have, right up to your most recent flight. It's a nice finishing touch that sends a great impression about your professionalism and attention to detail.

Give your logbooks a good once-over before you hand them in for the interview, regardless of what type you have. Keep an eye out for anything that may draw an interviewer's attention. Electronic logbooks do the math for you, but you must still be careful about entering bad data. A 2.0-hour flight can become a 20.0-hour flight if you misplace the decimal. These are the errors they look for in electronic logbooks. For manual logbooks, you'll want to check your entries *and* your math. A quick error check is to add single engine time plus multi engine time and make sure it equals the total.

One quick note about simulator time: Most companies do not want simulator time included in your totals. It's fine to keep a record of it, just keep it in a separate column from your total flight time.

Your logbooks are you on paper. If your logs look like you just pulled them out of a dumpster, you might as well have crawled out of the dumpster with them. Keeping your logbooks isn't about doing it the easiest way, the least time consuming way, or even the most hassle-free way (although some of the electronic solutions out there make it pretty easy). Your logbooks are an example of what kind of employee you will be. Are you the sloppy minimalist or the accurate professional? Make sure you are showing them the right picture.

Points to remember

✓ Have your most recent flight recorded, and the times totaled on the last page. Use pencil if your last entry doesn't complete the entire page.
✓ Check your flight time totals. One quick check interviewers can do is to see if your single engine time plus multi engine time equals your total time.
✓ Don't include simulator time in your total flight time.
✓ Before your interview, scan through your entries. Manual logbooks will generally have small mathematical errors; electronic logbooks can have large errors.
✓ Check for your signature at the bottom of each logbook page where it states you certify the flight times above are correct and accurate.
✓ If you've rebooted your logbooks at any point, you'll still want to bring your originals containing your training endorsements. Keep them in your briefcase to produce if requested.

Application package accuracy

All the components of your application package are going to be scrutinized, from the forms you fill out online, to your logbooks, and including the forms you have to fill out and sign on the day of the interview. You can bank on that fact. If you're not careful, accurate, and truthful when filling everything out, it can do you a lot more harm than good.

Interview Train Wreck #2

I was doing a logbook and paperwork review for a group of applicants to be interviewed. I totaled up one gentleman's logbook and compared it with the flight times he'd listed on his application. The numbers didn't add up. A red flag goes up, and suddenly this guy is in the spotlight before he's even stepped into the interview room. I handed everything to another recruiter, and asked them to run the numbers and make sure I hadn't hosed up the simple addition (always a possibility). The other recruiter came up with the same numbers I did. Even more unfortunately, the numbers in the guy's logbook (which he hadn't totaled himself on the last page, incidentally) didn't add up to the minimums required for the job. He was shy by about 20 hours.

As an interviewer, this paints you into a corner. When you meet with this person they could be a total rock star, but they've either lied on their application or made a major clerical error. You, as the interviewer, have to figure out what's really going on with the applicant. Even more of a problem, according to his logbook, the guy didn't have the required time to qualify for the job.

When I met him face to face, he was polite, had a firm handshake, neat suit, and all the basic requirements. We sat down and I said we needed to resolve a paperwork discrepancy. I neatly laid it all on the table and asked him what was going on with the flight times. He looked everything over for a minute, and then I saw realization dawn on his face. He explained that when he filled out the application he was flying about 50 hours a month. He figured on getting this interview in 2 months, so he added 100 hours to his total time on the application. According to his logbook, he'd only flown 80 hours, hence the 20-hour shortfall.

I told him I thought that was a reasonable explanation, and I didn't feel like he'd intentionally lied about his time, but without the 20 extra hours he'd added erroneously, he didn't meet the minimums. We couldn't consider his application at that time. I made a note in his file and said he could re-apply in 6 months (the minimum time between interviews) when he did meet the requirements.

Judging from his demeanor when he realized what was going on, I might as well have pulled the skin off my face and told him I was there to collect his soul. Believe me when I tell you that you don't ever want to put yourself in this situation. It sucks for everyone involved.

I'm sure that to this day, this guy tells people he has met evil incarnate, and that evil is named Rick Hogan. Who knows...maybe he's right.

Interview Train Wreck #3

I was sitting down with an applicant, doing the standard paperwork review at the beginning of the interview.

20

"Have you had any accidents, incidents, violations or convictions that aren't listed on your application?" I asked.

It was a standard line we asked everybody.

"No," the applicant replied. "Except I did get convicted for petty theft once. And assault."

Insert raised eyebrows, "OOOOkayyy. Did that happen recently?"

"No, it was about five years ago," he said.

"Why didn't you put that on your application right here, where it asks if you've ever been convicted of a crime?"

"I thought it sounded pretty bad," he reasoned, "so I wanted to explain it to you in person."

"OK. Well, since we're all here, what happened?"

Note: this isn't verbatim, but you'll get the idea, "I broke up with my girlfriend because she was seeing a friend of mine behind my back (somewhere in the back of my mind I imagine chanting as Jerry Springer walks around on a stage with his microphone). So, I was really upset, and one night I went and started taking the hubcaps off her car. I bought them for her, so it wasn't stealing. My friend, the one she was seeing, came out of her house and we got into a big fight. I threw one of the hubcaps at him, and they called the police. I got charged with everything, even though they were my hubcaps, really, and the guy came outside and started the fight."

"Seems like you got railroaded there," I said.

"Yeah. But I wanted to tell you in person so you could explain it to them so it wouldn't sound so bad. Can you explain it?"

"I'm making a note of it right now," I said as I started writing, 'Under no circumstances...'

"Cool, thanks."

"No, No. Thank you sir, thank you," I replied with complete sincerity.

Remember, interviews are like lightning strikes, and they don't happen that often. You don't want to burn one up by playing fast and loose with your application. Be accurate with your flight times as they stand right now. Don't project, embellish, or alter your flight times from what you have at the exact moment you are filling out the application. If the guy in the previous Interview Train Wreck had just waited one more month until he actually HAD the required time, he may have gotten the job. Instead, he ended up with a six-month delay before he could even apply again. It's not worth the gamble.

Leaving important items off your application can be just as detrimental as adding things on. If you fail to report something that an application specifically asks for, i.e. traffic violations, felony convictions, check ride failures, etc., thinking you'll just bring it up in the interview so you can explain it, you're putting yourself in an impossible situation. Report everything completely and honestly on your application. *Never lie on your paperwork or in an interview.*

If you're honest about everything and you get called for an interview, you're in great shape. The company has reviewed your paperwork and called you in, and they're OK with it. If there's something in your background they can't accept, they won't call. Be honest from the start and you won't have to waste your time or anyone else's interviewing for a job you can't get.

I've seen people get hired with all kinds of issues in their past: DUIs, busted check rides, accidents, incidents...the list goes on and on. No one is perfect, and everybody makes mistakes. The most effective way to mitigate issues from your past is to *clearly explain what happened and include as much documentation as possible*. Give a factual, unemotional, un-opinionated description of the incident and its outcome. Whether it's a violation or the fact that you failed your private pilot oral, take full responsibility. If the application asks for it or if the company contacts you, include as much documentation as you can. Stating on your application that you had a check ride failure, and then merely listing the date it happened provides nothing to the person reviewing your application. They will most likely assume the worst, your application will go to the circular file, and they'll move on. Stating you had a check ride failure, then giving a detailed description of why and further stating the subsequent re-check was successful, gives your application reviewer a lot more information to work with. Concentrate on being as detailed and thorough as the specific application will allow.

One last word of caution about trying to sneak something by: It's *very* unlikely you can do it in today's security climate. You may think you got something past, and you may make it all the way through training, but if the company finds out you lied on your initial application (even *years* down the road) they can and will fire you. This has been tried and proven over and over again. Negatives don't *necessarily* disqualify you unless you're not truthful about them. When you are applying, make sure you are *always* completely honest. Explaining a check ride failure isn't that big of a deal. Explaining that you got fired because you *lied* about a check ride failure *is* a big deal.

In order to be honest, you have to know what's on your record. The requirements for background checks on airline employees are pretty strict nowadays. Plan on having your FAA records, driving record, criminal history, and possibly even a credit report pulled on you. I personally know of pilots getting pulled out of new hire class and fired because something came back on a background check they hadn't disclosed during the application process. A good friend of mine got caught up in this frustrating situation for weeks because someone with his exact same name had multiple felony convictions. When the company pulled his criminal history, the felonies popped up. It took him time, money, and generated an immeasurable amount of stress to deal with this situation during new hire training.

You need to have the following information on hand and in order when you're ready to begin the application and interview process:

✓ Logbook
- Total and update your logbook.

✓ Current Passport

✓ College Transcripts

✓ Airman Certification Record
- Pull your copy to make sure there aren't any errors on your records. You can get a copy in the mail, but it may take several weeks to process. The forms can be found on the FAA (or applicable agency) website.

✓ Driving Record
- You should obtain a national driving record and check for accuracy. You can find a lot of companies online that provide this service.

✓ FCC License
- Most companies now require this license. Getting it is merely a matter of filling out the form and paying the fee. You can find it at the FCC.gov website.

- ✓ First Class Medical
  - Companies want to ensure you can obtain and maintain a first class medical, particularly if they don't give you their own evaluation. Plan on having a first class certificate.
- ✓ Previous Residence Information
  - Maintain a 10-year residence history for the background check.
- ✓ Previous Employment Information
  - Keep a 10-year history of previous employers, including contact information so you have it available and don't have to look it up each time. Include all periods of unemployment in your history as well.
- ✓ Training Records
  - It's helpful to keep a copy of your training records. If you have any check ride failures, you can include specific documentation on the event(s).
- ✓ Application Copies
  - Keep a hard-copy record of every application you fill out. You will need to refer back to it in the future for your interview. Many applications ask for similar information, so the information you use to fill out one will apply to other applications as well.

When you are ready to begin the application process, pull this information together so you don't get any surprises. If there's an error on your records (i.e. your drug smuggling conviction is incorrectly listed as human trafficking) you can start the process of getting it corrected immediately. Depending on what the error is, it can be a lengthy process. If you get an interview before the error is corrected, you can alert the company beforehand that there is an error on your records, but you're in the process of fixing it. Once you run your background check and it comes back correct, keep everything for your records. If the company gets something different on a check they run, you can produce your own records. You'll have proof that there is an error. This can also help with the correction process.

Points to remember

✓ Always be completely honest on your résumé and application.
✓ If you have issues that must be disclosed, provide as much detail and documentation as the application will allow. Bring any and all documentation to the interview.
✓ Have the records and documentation listed in this section ready and available. You need to know what information is contained in your records and ensure it's correct.

Bring what they ask for

Not having everything you've been asked to bring to an interview can be an immediate showstopper.

When we invited an applicant for an interview, he was sent a packet with a detailed list of required copies and completed forms to bring with him. I happened to know exactly what was on the list because I helped put the invitation packet together.

The idea behind the invitation packet was that between the briefing, written test, interview, simulator evaluation, and drug test, we were tight on time to get everything completed in one day. Filling out all the paperwork, and making copies of licenses and documents wasn't part of the itinerary (particularly some of the background check forms that took some time to complete).

I sat down with a gentleman in the interview room and asked for his paperwork, which was how every interview started. Everything was supposed to be collected and put in the applicant's folder, along with the interview evaluation paperwork that would be filled out over the course of the day.

"Can I please get the background check forms and copies we asked you to bring in?" I asked.

"I didn't have time to get copies of everything," the applicant warned, as he started rummaging through his brief case.

"OK, let's see what you do have."

The applicant produced all of the completely blank forms and no copies.

"Right. So...when did you get the interview packet?" I asked.

"About a week ago, but I've been flying a lot since then. I thought I could just fill them out here."

I noticed the invitation letter in the jumble of blank forms he'd just dumped out on the table. I pulled it out of the pile and pointed to the first sentence of the first paragraph that read: Congratulations on being selected. Please complete the included forms and bring copies of the following documents with you to the interview.

"Did you notice on this invitation letter where it asks you to complete all these forms beforehand?" I asked, genuinely curious.

The applicant, now sensing he may have made an error in judgment said, "Here, I'll just fill them out while you ask me some questions."

At this point in almost any interview I usually turn green, grow to four times my normal size, and destroy the building around us. Interview complete.

With the possible exception of certain sadomasochistic niche fetish cults (hey, to each his own), nobody *likes* paperwork, electronic or otherwise. In the recruiting department, they want a very long and detailed data trail on each applicant, particularly if they're hired. That way, two years down the road when they catch one of your interviewees smuggling heroin out of Mexico, the chief pilot can scream at you, "Why didn't you figure out he was a heroin smuggler in the interview!?"

Certain forms are required for every interview with a US company. You will fill out previous employer verification, training record requests, National Driving Record, and FAA records requests along with maybe a few others.

After you deal with the standard forms, companies will have specific forms with information they want to see. Sometimes it will be an application form or it might be a flight time summary sheet asking for obscure breakdowns of your flight time (how much single engine overwater night simulated instrument time do you have?). This is the stuff you really want to spend some time on. Whether it's online or an actual paper form you are filling out, keep in mind that the people reviewing this information have seen these forms hundreds of times. If you fill it out incorrectly or leave something blank, they will notice immediately. Does making a mistake automatically disqualify you from the job? Not necessarily. You will start out with a much stronger first impression, however, if you don't have any errors on your paperwork.

How do you ensure you fill everything out correctly? *Take your time* and *double check your work* as carefully as the online portions of the process. If you have the forms in advance of the actual interview, it helps having someone else check it over, if you can. Finding errors in your own writing is twice as hard as finding them in someone else's.

Part of taking your time is not waiting until the night before your interview to fill everything out and get it all together. If you're "flying a lot" (see Interview Train Wreck #3), make some time to spend on your paperwork. Put off checking in with all 1500 of your Facebook friends, and just make time to do it right. It will pay off in the end. Read every line, check over your responses, and make sure they are all correct. After you've filled everything out, wait a day, and then check it all over one more time.

I interviewed a guy who checked a box on his application that said he had been convicted of a felony, but didn't list when or what the conviction was. Turns out he just checked the wrong box. Not a deal breaker necessarily, but it's nice to be accurate when you're talking about felony convictions. How do you avoid making these kinds of errors? Not to be repetitive, but *take your time* and *double-check your work*.

The company you're interviewing with will send you, either electronically or via snail mail, a list of everything they want you to have on interview day. It may take you a few days to get everything together depending on the nature of what they want. As you acquire each piece of information, cross if off the list they sent you. Before you leave for your interview, go through the list one last time, checking off each item as you place it in your briefcase. You don't want to find out you forgot your college transcripts when you're sitting in the interview hot seat.

Points to remember

✓ Make sure you have all the paperwork the company has requested, and that it's all filled out correctly. Take your time filling out the paperwork, and double check your work. Have another person check it over for mistakes, if possible.
✓ Cross off each requested paperwork item as you acquire it. Before you leave for your interview, go through the list again, checking off each item as you place it in your briefcase.

Recommendations

The application process has evolved, to be sure, so are recommendation letters still important? You'd better believe it. Some companies put more weight on them than others, but in every case it's better to have a letter on file than not.

For online applications, there is a form current employees can usually fill out on your behalf, and it will be tied to your application package electronically. Try to have your contact give you a hard copy of what they've submitted, and keep it with your records. It helps to know what exactly they've written when you get called for an interview. If you're applying to a company that still uses paper, have your recommendation writer submit the letter to the appropriate people, then be sure to get a copy for your records.

Having a recommendation on file is a significant credit to your application package, so much so that if there is a company you are really trying to get noticed by, you need to make a point of getting one. Don't know anyone at the company you're aiming for? You need to start networking: meaning figure out a way to get in contact with someone (preferably a pilot) employed there. Many, many people aren't comfortable trying to establish a relationship with a total stranger for professional reasons. They view it as "schmoozing," "kissing a@$," or some other negative term, and that's great for you, because all those people will be behind you in the interview pile. If you're not networking in the airline business, it's like shooting yourself in the kneecap, because everyone else is.

Also good news for you: Networking has never been easier than it is today. With the amount of social media options available at any given moment, you should have no problem connecting with someone, online at least, and online is enough. Whether you went to a major university or a small Podunk flight school, odds are someone from there has gone on to work for a company you'd like to be at. If not, you probably know someone who knows someone whose third uncle removed is an airline pilot. All you need is an email address, telephone number, Facebook account... something. LinkedIn is a huge resource for establishing professional relationships. If you're in a quandary about how to get the ball rolling, start there.

Here's why networking is so effective in the airline industry: Pilots love talking about their jobs. Most pilots *are pilots* because they love flying, and it's very rare to find someone who got into the profession strictly for the paycheck. It's easy to forge a relationship with someone when you share a common passion. Second only to flying itself, pilots love talking about their particular job and or company. Almost without exception, most pilots will go out of their way to help someone working their way up. It makes them feel important, for one thing. Beyond that, there is an almost universal sense of genuinely wanting to help others on their career paths. If you can make a connection, and not act like a total sycophantic a-hole, then they will more than likely be willing to help you out in some way, even if you've never met in real life. He or she may give you some advice, and that may be the extent of it, but they may offer to go a little further, as far as recommending you at some point down the road. The longer the relationship you establish with this person, the more help they will be willing to provide.

If and when you make a connection with someone, use some judgment.

The first sentence you say (or write) shouldn't be, "Hey, write me a recommendation letter!"

Start by explaining your situation, then simply ask their opinion on the best way to get hired at XYZ airlines. I can almost guarantee they'll be happy to share their view on your career track; it just takes asking the question.

Example:

"Hi John. My name is Harrowitz McNickel. I went to school with your nephew's friend Winston Churchill. I really want to fly for Super-Mega Airlines someday. I know you're a pilot there, and I was wondering if you had any suggestions about what I could do to make that happen."

Simply connecting with someone, particularly online, does *not* mean they will immediately start opening doors for you. That's not how this whole process works. Think of this whole process, from first filling out an online application to starting new hire training, as a marathon, not a sprint. If you lay the groundwork for solid relationships and make serious efforts to expand your professional network, it won't necessarily pay off tomorrow (or even the day *after* tomorrow), but it *will* eventually. I'll give you a money-back guarantee on that. Think of networking as an investment in your future, and a very important one at that.

Recommendation letters can be a critical component to getting hired. That's the reason it's not always easy to get one. Don't spare any effort to find a way to stack the odds in your favor.

Points to remember

✓ Network whenever you can, as often as you can. Having a recommendation is one way to set yourself apart from the pack.

Stand out from the crowd

How can you distinguish yourself from the thousands of other pilots out there grinding out as much flight time as they can month after month? Particularly, how can you do it in a point-based application system that is specifically created to equalize everyone? By racking up as many points as you can, of course. The benefit to this is that it works for any type of application process, whether it's point based or not.

Build your résumé

The best way to build your résumé is by holding positions of additional responsibility at the company you're currently working for. First off, you're trying to score as many points as you can on your application and make it to the top of the heap. Beyond that, at some point a real person will look at your application package. As a recruiter, once you review your 500th résumé or application, they all start to look the same. A little more or less flight time, ratings from this school instead of that school...that's the only difference you'll see 90% of the time. What starts catching your eye are responsibilities a pilot has above and beyond just flying the line. You notice things like pilots teaching CRM, interviewing applicants, or developing training curriculum. Jobs that go beyond flight time set you apart from your peers and will catch the eye of potential employers.

You should *always* be on the lookout for ways to advance your career outside normal seniority progression. Anything you can put on your application and résumé that will make you *just a little* more qualified than someone who hasn't done those things will help.

An opening will pop up for some position somewhere, and when it does, jump on it. At some point your company will need CRM facilitators, or they'll need volunteers for the incident response team. If they need sim instructors, or IOE pilots, apply! Will these additional duties require you to give up some free time? Yes. Will you get paid more for doing them? Maybe, but in some cases you won't. So, why do it? Because when Delta Airlines starts hiring for the first time in 4 years, they're going to have 10,000 applications on file before the window closes. I've heard of companies getting so many applications so quickly their servers crash. Probably half of these applicants will have an internal letter of recommendation. You need to set yourself apart. Anything you can put on your résumé/application that distinguishes you from the other slugs out there robotically building flight time is worth its weight in gold.

Here is a personal example:

Like many lucky things in my life, I stumbled into the pilot-recruiting thing. With the advent of regional jets, the airline I was at suddenly needed to triple its size. A guy I flew with (very senior captain) was tasked with formally setting up a "pilot recruiting department." I must have been having a better than normal day when we flew together, because for some reason he decided to call me out of the blue.

"We need people right away," was the thrust of the conversation.

Since I was in fact available, I was immediately qualified and accepted. The rest is history.

I have *always* been the low-time guy at the interview and in new-hire training. Why do companies notice my application over someone else's? Many applicants had more flight time and more recommendation letters than me. The answer to getting noticed is not *all* about flight time and recommendation letters. The fact that I worked in the recruiting department has caught the attention of *every* company I have *ever* interviewed with. I know this, for a fact, because it has come up in *every single* interview. Did I mention *every*?

Jump on any opportunity that you see. If you have one position and a better one opens up, take a step up the ladder. It may be more work and you may not particularly like the job. It may disrupt your online social networking time, but you can't put a price tag on this kind of experience. If you want to advance your career as far as possible, make it happen.

"Wait a tic," you may be thinking to yourself. "I work for Joe Bob's Podunk Flight School, or BFE Charter Operation. We don't have any of those programs or departments."

Even better.

Walk up to your chief pilot and say, "Excuse me, Captain Courageous? I was thinking we could really use an incident response plan (insert applicable program of your choice). Just in case -you know- we have an incident or accident, it would give us a step-by-step procedure to follow. Would you mind if I put something together?"

Pretty much any program that improves safety, ensures regulatory compliance, or decreases costs will work. I have yet to hear any supervisor declining an offer for free work. Captain Courageous can now go to his boss with tangible evidence that he's enhancing the operation, not just updating his Facebook page on an hourly basis. Developing any kind of program benefits everyone: You, your boss, and the company. Win, win, win.

"Wait another tic," you may say. "I have no idea how to put together an incident response plan."

I typed "aviation incident response plan" into Google and got 7 (that I counted) different plans, all downloadable in PDF format. Download them, take a look, and plug in your applicable information.

Change the program around just enough to make it yours. Remember, imitation is the highest form of flattery. Dress it up a little with your company specifics, some snappy graphics, and then hand in your plan.

Now, go to your résumé and add a new entry under the "Experience" heading. It should say something like *Incident Response Program Manager.* Under your duties write, *developed and implemented incident response program.* Voilà.

If you show some initiative, new opportunities will find their way to you. The Chief Pilot will come to you the next time he needs something that's outside the box. And guess what? That gives you another entry for your résumé as well.

Eventually, someone at the company you're shooting for will say, "Hey, we need to interview this CRM facilitator, incident response, simulator instructor, and IOE evaluator person."

That's when all the effort will pay off.

Points to remember

✓ Develop your résumé beyond just building flight time. Take on additional duties and responsibilities whenever you can. If there aren't any available, make your own.

Non-flying jobs

Every company out there loves to promote from within, and they also want to feel like you're applying to them because you really want to work there. You want to avoid the impression you shot-gunned applications everywhere in the world, and they're the first to reply.

There are a lot of jobs at airlines that you can work part-time, while you're still building flight time, and establish a long-term relationship with the company. It carries a lot of weight to sit in an interview and say you wanted to work for XYZ airlines since you were a baggage handler several years ago. They absolutely love that kind of thing. You may not enjoy driving the turd-hearse and emptying lavs as much as you do flying, but working a job like that at a career goal company can pay big dividends down the road. Plus, it builds up your immune system.

I know a guy who worked as a package sorter at one of the major delivery companies every Christmas. He got his ratings, built his time, and when he met the requirements, he applied for a pilot job. They could not have been happier that he began his career as a ground employee and came back to be a pilot. They even offered to hire him directly into management. In addition to the management offer, the tone of his interview was totally different from the tone of mine. His interview was a friendly, "welcome back," while mine was confrontational (we'll talk about different interview styles later). Anything you can do to stack the deck in your favor is never a bad idea.

Not everyone is going to be in a position to do this kind of thing, but if you're looking for a second job, it might as well be one that can help your career down the road. Most entry-level flying jobs require some type of supplemental income just to cover your ramen noodles and hamburger helper expenses. I used to finish a trip at around 9 A.M. as a first officer and then go to my other job working the desk at a local fitness center. Welcome to paying dues in professional aviation. While the fitness center gave me a free gym membership and a lot of eye candy, my time would have been better spent making my résumé stronger. A part-time job that opens doors down the road is worth more than watching Pilates classes come and go.

Establish an application history

At some point during your interview, they're going to want to know when and why you decided to work for their company. Being able to point to the fact that you've been applying for the last 4 years proves to your interviewers you have more than a passing interest in working for their company.

To establish an application history, submit your résumé or application *as soon as you meet the minimums to apply*. I meet a lot of people who want to work for a particular airline, but haven't even submitted their paperwork.

The first question I always ask is, "Why not? You can't get the job if you don't apply."

"I'm not competitive."

"I'm waiting for my friend who works there to submit it for me."

"I'm too busy."

If you are even considering applying somewhere, get your info to them as soon as you can. The longer your application package is on file, the more chance you have to get called. And the longer you have something on file, the more it shows you really want to work there. Don't wait.

All flight time is not equal

All flight time is good, but some is better. This section is written from the perspective of viewing every job you have that isn't your career goal as merely a step toward achieving that end. Maintaining an upward career track requires continually evaluating what the best type of flight time is for you right now, and what you need to do to get it.

Say you've got 2000 hours giving dual instruction in a C172. Is another 1000 hours in that operation going to make you more marketable to an employer? What about 3000? 10,000? Probably not. When you've got 1000 hours in your logbook at any "time builder" position, it's time to start looking seriously at stepping up, if you can.

Should I keep this nifty banner-towing gig or move on to flying checks at night? I'm flying a rich guy around in the back of a Pilatus. My time is all turbine PIC, so would it really help to take a regional FO job? Deciding which type of flight time is more valuable can be tricky. There's a "know when to hold 'em and know when to fold 'em" component (as well as some luck) that factors in. One thing you should *always* be doing is ranking the value of the flight time you're building, and asking yourself if it's the best you can be doing.

So, the $2 million dollar question is, what's the best time you can get? In the "build your résumé" section, we talked about how airlines love it when you take on more responsibility, and you can apply that to building flight time as well. The flight time that is generally ranked highest by airlines is: operating as a check airman or IOE instructor. Why? You're not only operating the aircraft in daily operations, you're evaluating someone or training someone in said environment. As anyone who's filled these roles before can tell you, they can be a lot of work, and you have a lot of liability with each person you sign off. More responsibility = more value.

What about the type of operation? Airlines typically like to hire from a diverse background: some civilian, some military, some corporate, etc. In their view, it keeps the new hire "gene pool" fresh.

Personally, I think you can't go wrong with airline time, because it's apples to apples.

"Is this person going to be able to get up to speed on our current operations? Are we going to have to train them on how to do things at an airline?"

If you're already logging 100 hours of airline time a month, that question is easily answered. If you've got a military background already, and (depending on your situation) you reach the point where you can start logging some civilian airline time, you're checking *all* the boxes. Same with corporate; if you've got several thousand hours of corporate operation, transitioning to airline operations will make you more valuable than someone who doesn't.

When you get down to aircraft type, things get a little simpler: Multi engine is better than single engine. Crew operations are better than single pilot. Turbine is better than piston. PIC is better than second in command (SIC).

All that seems pretty cut and dried while you're sitting here reading it, envisioning your career track as a rocket heading straight up all the time. Unfortunately, that's not always how it goes. You may get stuck somewhere for a while, and then you get comfortable, and then it becomes a question of lifestyle.

"I'm a senior FO, getting weekends and holidays off. Do I really want to go be a captain sitting on reserve five days a week?"

Switching companies, and even seats at the same company, isn't necessarily fun, easy, or stress-free. It's a lot of work, but as a wise man once said, a rolling stone gathers no moss. And you don't want to be a moss-covered stone, right?

How do you decide whether to stay where you are or move on? Sit down in a quiet room and listen to the small voice in the back of your head. You'll be surprised how often that voice is right:

1. More responsibility is always better. PIC is better than SIC. PIC as an instructor pilot is better than just straight PIC. PIC as a designated examiner is better than instructor. See the trend?

2. The bigger and faster the aircraft, the better; heavy jet, jet, large turboprop, turboprop, all the way down to C172. If you have 1000 hours PIC in a turboprop, start looking for a position in a jet. If you have that time in a jet, start looking for heavy jet.

A good benchmark to reach as quickly as possible is 1000 hours of turbine PIC. That opens the most application doors. If that turbine PIC is also jet PIC, most of the remaining doors will open, too. There are some companies that won't follow the standard rules. When you start looking at foreign jobs and/or direct entry captain stuff, it gets a little more complicated and specific. Whatever your case, if your current job is a "time-building" job, as soon as you get 1000 hours PIC in the top equipment they have available, it's time to start looking for the next move.

Having said all the above, you will want to take a hard, unemotional look at the company you're thinking of moving to very carefully. They may offer you a job flying as a 777 captain, but if they declare bankruptcy and shut the doors before you get out of new hire training, you can take that job offer into the bathroom and...well, you get the idea. Anytime you switch companies, you're rolling the dice. Things might look great right now, but can come grinding to a halt with alarming speed. Here's a real life example:

I worked with a guy who was less than a year away from upgrading to captain on the CRJ. He knew I did some career counseling stuff, so he came to me with a question.

He had a job offer as a 737 First Officer from a startup company called AccessAir.

AccessAir had 4 airplanes and operated between New York and Los Angeles through their hub in Des Moines, IA. Having actually grown up in the vicinity of Des Moines, that sounded like an odd business model to me, but hey, stranger things and all that...

"What do you think I should do?" he asked me. "Should I take the job?"

"Is AccessAir someplace you want to spend your career or are you just looking to build time?"

"Build time. I want to go to Delta," he said.

"I don't see the advantage to switching companies," I said. "The CRJ PIC you're close to getting is worth more than 737 SIC anyway. I would get your 1000 PIC before you seriously look at leaving here."

"But the upgrade at AccessAir is only 6 months! I can get my 1000 hours of PIC on the 737, which would be *a lot* better than the RJ."

I said, "Listen, if you've got three birds in a tree, and one of them poops in your hand...wait...that's not right. OK, forget that part. Upgrade here is almost a sure thing. You're rolling the dice on this AccessAir place. I'm not sure it's worth the gamble."

"OK," he said. "I'll think it over."

So he did, and two weeks later he was starting class at AccessAir (which shows how much weight my opinion carried, I suppose).

At this point, you may be wondering who AccessAir is and why you've never heard of them. You've never heard of them because they declared bankruptcy and totally liquidated about 3 months after this person went to work there. Then he was stuck re-applying to get another regional job; the exact same job he left 3 months ago. Only now, instead of captain upgrade being less than a year away, it was 3-5 years away.

So, where was the payoff for going to AccessAir? By his own admission, this person only wanted to go to AccessAir to build time to get to Delta. Was going to AccessAir really going to help him realize his dream of getting to Delta that much faster? I didn't think so, but he did. Personally, I like to deal in absolutes whenever possible.

Assuming AccessAir would have kept operating, is 737 PIC time more valuable than CRJ PIC time? Maybe a little. Maybe. It's bigger for sure, a little faster, and there's the perception it's a real airliner rather than a just a "regional jet" (I can say that because I have a lot of time in a regional jet). Not enough of a difference, however, to justify a risky move like this was.

Carefully weigh your options anytime you're considering switching companies to build bigger and better time. I'm all for taking a gamble, but make sure the payoff is worth the risk

Points to remember

- ✓ Build the highest quality flight time you can as quickly as possible. Shoot for 1000 PIC turbine ASAP.
- ✓ Put a lot of thought into decisions about chasing bigger and better equipment. The fastest way to the highest quality flight time might be staying put. There is risk associated with any job switch.

Avoid the stagnation zone

I was in the top 25% of the seniority list at my regional airline, getting great schedules, making decent pay, and generally taking it all for granted. I was grumbling to and from work every day because it wasn't where I wanted to be (I know... waaaah... poor me).

I had several thousand hours of PIC, and had been doing hiring for a few years. Deciding I'd gotten everything I could from this company in terms of career advancement, it was time to move on. I took a job with a non-scheduled ACMI carrier flying a 747-400 all around the world. I had always wanted to fly that airframe, but the job itself was a significant pay cut, a huge quality of life hit, and everyone generally looked at me like I was crazy. Why did I take it? I listened to the little voice inside, and it said that more regional jet PIC wasn't going to help me get where I wanted to be, but some wide body international might.

I started class with the new company, and on day one they said they needed more bodies. Anyone we recommended would be brought in for an interview almost immediately (remember that networking section?). That was exciting. I couldn't wait to get back and tell all my friends. Catching up with them at a poker game that weekend, I told them what the deal was. There were basically open interviews for anybody who wanted to come; just let me know and I'd set it up.

There were 5 guys at that game, each of them at the same regional airline as me. They all literally laughed in my face.

The general consensus was, "Who wants to be gone for 17 days at a time? How do you even pack a bag for that? That job sucks, and you're an idiot for going there."

That response was fine, and maybe I was. I spent the rest of the poker game wondering if I was making a huge mistake, but what was done was done, and all I could do was press forward.

Flash forward a couple of years, and that ACMI job led to bigger and better things, as I'd hoped it would. Hiring in the airline industry literally ground to a halt. All those guys at the poker game had now been stuck at that regional airline for nearly 10 years, and were dying to get out. One ended up taking a job with that same ACMI carrier he had turned up his nose at years before. It was the same job he could have had (years before) if he hadn't let himself get so comfortable at the regional job he didn't want to leave. Another guy actually interviewed there, but wasn't successful, partly because jobs were much more scarce when he interviewed and the company could be as picky as they wanted with whom they hired.

I mentioned at the beginning of this book that opportunities don't come along in the industry *that* often. I consider myself having had many more opportunities than most, and I can count them on my fingers with a few left over. If an opportunity drops in your lap, like someone saying, "Hey, I can get you an interview at this place tomorrow," you need to at least consider it. The job may not be something you ever considered doing, but take some time to mull it over before you laugh in someone's face. You'll be surprised how your short-term career expectations shift three to five years from now.

Don't sabotage yourself while building time

I've been trying to resist it for a long time, but my inner nerd is dying to come out. I'm going to make a reference to the butterfly effect. The principle relates to chaos theory, which in this career can feel like it's swirling all around you at times. The butterfly effect is the theory that a butterfly flapping its wings today sets in motion a chain of events that at some point in the future will cause a tornado. I don't know if that really happens or not, but the theory of it is important. What the butterfly effect means to you is that a decision which seems small and insignificant now can turn into a tornado down the road. That tornado can suck your career into it and spit it out as a twisted and unrecognizable mess. As you're building time and working toward your career goals, keep the butterfly effect in mind.

Anytime you're faced with a decision, whether it's a job switch or figuring out the right operational course of action, think of risk versus reward. Be wary of shady companies with super-quick upgrade times. If upgrade and advancement times are uncharacteristically low at some company you've never heard of, there is probably a reason. You can get good flight time quickly at places like that, but you need to guard your airman certificates like the precious documents they are. You don't want to end up dragging a boat anchor around on your record in the form of a violation. Here's another example:

A guy I went to flight school with took a job at a shady night freight operation flying a decent-sized turboprop. It seemed like a good opportunity to fly a turbine powered aircraft in a multi-crew environment. All in all it was pretty high quality time for a low time guy just starting out. He upgraded to captain in no time, and was working toward his 1000 PIC turbine. Everything was looking good and he was on a good track.

The downside of this particular company was they were always pushing pilots to bend the rules. Don't worry about writing up that item, we'll fix it in the morning. Don't worry about how much all that stuff weighs, you'll be fine. We know the weather isn't technically "legal," but you can make it in. There was pressure coming from the wrong directions, and this guy didn't make any waves and kept the aircraft moving.

He justified all these small compromises to himself because he was building turbine engine PIC time quickly. He kept thinking he only had to put up with it just long enough to get his time and get out. Then, he could put the place behind him, move on to bigger and better things, and never have to worry about it again.

As it turned out, the FAA got wind that a lot of sketchy stuff was going on at this place. One day they rode into town and took a hard look at everything going on, and they were not pleased. Long story short: for all his effort to get his time quickly and move on, he now had a shiny new violation following him around. The last I heard, he was still flying that turboprop.

I'm approaching this section from a career advancement standpoint, but there is the *much* more important safety aspect to these decisions that I could write an entire separate book on. Yes, it's true you don't want to get a violation. *Much* more important is that you, the people who care about you, and the people in the back of the plane who are *depending* on you, don't want your aircraft to end up in a smoking pile of wreckage. There's a *reason* for making good decisions, and the primary one isn't career advancement. Later in this book, we're going to spend a great deal of time on building an effective decision making framework that will help you give good interview answers. That same framework will also keep you out of trouble in the real world, both legally *and* physically. For just right now, we're only talking about job implications.

Can you get a top-tier job with a violation? It's possible, but it is an issue that will be addressed by any potential employer. There are a lot of pilots out there with clean records; you'll need to convince the company you're worth the risk over someone without any baggage. If you have something negative following you around on your record, the first thing you need to know is be honest about it when applying. Don't be vague, coy, or in any way not direct and up front about your history. If you are clear and direct about issues like this during your application, and you get called in for an interview, the company is saying to you, "We have reviewed this, and if you have a reasonable explanation we can live with it." If you're not up front about it, it will immediately disqualify you.

Next, you need to put some time between yourself and the event. Everyone makes mistakes. If you operate with no accidents, incidents, or violations for a significant period of time, that demonstrates you've probably learned from yours. If and when the event comes up in an interview, the most important thing to do is take responsibility. Don't try to blame someone else or make an excuse. Relay the event in a clear, concise, and direct way. Describe what happened, why it happened, *what you learned*, and *how it changed your behavior* so it won't happen again. Learning from mistakes is a big part of being a good pilot, and if you can use this as an example of getting something positive from something negative, you've handled it the best way possible.

A violation is a big millstone to carry around your neck. The best way to handle violations in interviews is to avoid getting one at all costs. There are a lot of pressures out there, not necessarily coming from the right direction. Again, not even accounting for the safety aspect, if you find yourself in a questionable situation, remember this: it's much easier to explain in an interview that you left a previous employer because you refused to fly unsafe/illegal aircraft than describing what you learned from your violation.

Points to remember

✓ Building time is important, but keeping a clean record is more important. Think about the butterfly effect anytime you're faced with a tough choice: don't let a small issue turn into something huge you'll have to deal with for the rest of your career.

Part 2

Physical presentation

Eventually (and in some cases unexpectedly) all your work will pay off and the interview call will come. The call will probably come when you least expect it. You may receive it during the most inconvenient circumstances possible. I once received a call for an interview in the middle of a family cookout surrounded by laughing, yelling, music-filled chaos. Try playing that one cool. If you are in job hunt mode and you receive a call from a number you don't recognize, particularly if you're not in a good setting to field a career-altering call, it may be best to let it go to voicemail.

You get the call. You schedule the interview. The job is now yours to lose. But lose it you will not, as Yoda would say. In the days leading up to your interview you now have a new job. That job is called interview preparation. If you properly prepare for your interview, you have done everything you can to ensure a positive outcome. The key is how to be properly prepared, which is why you're suffering through your 150th book related to aviation. We will cover, in the painstaking detail that only a book about flying could contain, how to properly prepare for your interview.

You've done a lot of work to get to the point of scheduling this interview. Now is the time you need to kick it into high gear. Even if it's not a job you're sure you want, don't blow off the interview and just show up. If you don't fully commit to getting ready, someday when you are interviewing for a job you do want you're going to remember getting shot down in this one. It will add stress to an already stressful situation. Give it 110% or don't do it; nothing in between. If you're on the fence about a job but you've decided to do the interview, get the job first then decide if you want it. Not vice versa.

Looks aren't everything, but they're a lot

I know we live in a society that says everyone is a unique snowflake and looks aren't important. That is *not* the case in an interview setting, however. It's not necessarily a beauty contest, but you absolutely, positively, WILL be judged on how you look. Just come to terms with it.

First impressions are formed almost instantaneously. Some studies say they are formed in as little as 4 seconds. You can't say a whole lot in 4 seconds, so what does that tell you about where the majority of the first impression you're sending is coming from? It comes from how you're dressed, how you walk, how you shake someone's hand…every visual aspect you present will be consciously and subconsciously judged by your interviewers in just a few short seconds. And you've only got one chance to do it right.

At its heart, the interview process is and always will be very subjective. That means the interviewer's *opinion* ultimately can and will override all the other data they collect. You can know every technical answer and regurgitate obscure bits of aviation trivia until you're blue in the face, but if your interviewers don't get a good feeling about you, all your effort is wasted. An opinion will be formed based on your first handshake, how you enter the room and sit down at the table, and how you act upon the initial introduction. This is your chance to win them over to your side. You need your interviewers to pull for you instead of against you.

Interviewers subconsciously (or even consciously) work to one of two ends almost immediately after meeting you:

1. First impression is positive, they like you, and build a case to hire you.

2. First impression is negative, they don't like you, and build a case to not hire you.

Giving marginal performances in the simulator or on the written test can be mitigated if the interviewers like you. I've seen it happen over and over again. Vice versa, you can have a stellar simulator performance, ace the written test, but if you come across like Attila the Hun in a business suit, nothing else will matter. You can have every qualification there is, including a lunar landing, but if you show up in flip flops and start picking your nose during the interview, you won't get the job. You need your interviewers to think of the reasons to hire you, not reasons to reject you.

The first impression your interviewers form may be the single most important factor in determining whether you get the job or not. Let's talk about ways to make your interviewers work for you instead of against you.

Dress like a professional

Despite a lot of other opinions to the contrary, being a pilot is a professional job. You've got to look the part if you want a top-tier job.

Interview Train Wreck #5

I stood at the front of a classroom, getting ready to give the welcome briefing to a room containing about ten applicants. I always liked doing the briefing. I enjoyed giving them a warm welcome and looking at the hopeful and excited faces perched on top of their crisply pressed interview suits.

[Read the following in Dr. Seuss's voice...]

There was a black suit.

There was a blue suit.

There was a grey suit.

There was a plaid shirt.

Wait a second...plaid shirt doesn't rhyme with black suit. Something here is not the same. Which one doesn't belong?

Almost all the applicants were wearing very professional suit and tie combinations. One applicant, however, had opted for a plaid shirt, paisley tie, Dockers, and boat shoes.

This poor guy was nervously glancing around and appeared to be trying to shrink down under the table in order to disappear from sight. When he saw me look at him, instead of meeting my gaze and smiling (like the other applicants) he immediately looked down and began intently studying his fingers.

So, where does this leave him for the upcoming interview that day? Did I decide then and there he wasn't getting the job based on his attire? Not necessarily. But, this gentleman immediately had a lot of obstacles to overcome. Before the welcome briefing has even started, I'm formulating some questions this applicant needs to answer.

Maybe his suit got stolen out of his hotel room last night and this was the best he could do on short notice. I could live with that.

Or maybe there is a total disconnect between what he thinks looks professional and what others do. That would be a big problem. Pilots (it doesn't matter if you're talking cargo or passenger) are a very visible representation of a company to the public. If the pilots look like crap, the airline looks like crap.

Whatever was going on with this applicant, it was something that needed to be resolved. The last thing anyone wants on interview day is to start out with both feet in the grave. Because of what he chose to wear to his interview, this guy was definitely standing in the hole.

I got him in the interview, and I didn't even have to say anything about how he was dressed. I'm not sure if he was uncomfortable because of the plaid shirt, or if he was just having a really off day, but the interview was terrible. He couldn't come up with a good answer to anything, even the questions that didn't have right or wrong answers. I believe this all goes back to his attire. If you're showing up in a plaid shirt and paisley tie, it's because you don't take the interview seriously. If you don't take the interview seriously, you're just wasting everyone's time.

I had a great suit when I was in college. I referred to it simply as "The Black Suit." Now that I think back, it wasn't actually a suit per se. It was a black suit jacket that matched a black pair of pants, and matched probably isn't the right word. They were both black (or at least similar shades of black) even though they were made out of different materials. From a distance the ensemble looked great, kind of like that fake city in North Korea.

When I got the call to interview with a Legacy carrier in the early 2000s, I was beyond excited. I immediately started gathering things together for the big day. My wife asked what I was going to wear, and I found the question in itself puzzling.

"The Black Suit," I replied without hesitation. I only had ONE suit, after all.

"You don't have a black suit," she said, rubbing her temples as if a migraine was setting in. "You have a jacket and pants that don't match. Go get a suit."

I started to argue on behalf of The Black Suit, because it was kind of like an old friend. The Black Suit had always been right there for me at weddings, Christmas parties, and anniversary dinners over the years. I was formulating this argument when I looked into her steely eyes and relented immediately.

I didn't completely understand her logic, but I trusted it nonetheless.

"I'll go get one the day before I leave," I consented.

She let out a long sigh and stared at the ceiling as if she were praying. Grabbing her car keys, she said, "Come with me."

We drove to an upscale mall, which I only set foot in previously to visit the food court. I could see the bill for this suit increasing exponentially, but she would not be dissuaded. She dragged me like a petulant child through the mall to the most expensive men's clothing store I'd ever been in. We explained the situation to the salesman. He brought out a selection of what were, admittedly, very nice looking suits, each one costing more than my first car.

We settled on a charcoal grey one. I had it fitted and picked it up several days later. I even picked out a nice red tie that cost more than all the other ties I owned combined. I hated parting with that much cash, but after trying on the newly fitted suit and tie I noticed something important: it looked a lot better than The Black Suit ever did. I've had

The Grey Suit we bought that day for nearly 10 years now, and it has more than paid for itself. I consider it an investment.

You may already have a nice suit. If you do, I'm sure you've probably figured out by this point in your life that you want to wear it to the interview. I related my personal story for two reasons:

1. If you haven't spared the time or expense to get a GOOD suit, it's time. It's an investment in your career, and your future.
2. You cannot underestimate how important your appearance is on interview day.

Like I said at the beginning of this section, your interviewers will form an opinion about you within the first 4 seconds of meeting. It's like going on a blind date with the most probing, judgmental, fickle person you've ever met. Your visual presentation weighs heavily. That doesn't mean you have to look like a model, but you DO have to look like someone who can effectively take command of an airliner.

Most airline uniforms are traditional and conservative. You want your interviewers to be able to picture you in their company's uniform. The rule for suits applies for both men and women. Pick a suit that's conservative and traditional in color and style (darker colors being better, in my professional opinion) and *make sure it fits you well.* Don't borrow a suit from your sibling who's almost the same size as you. The suit should be tailored for you and you alone. The legs and arms should not be too short, nor should the pants and jacket be too tight.

For ladies, I would recommend a pantsuit. I've seen women interview in skirt suits, and while I don't think they look bad, you're not going to be wearing a skirt with your uniform. It's best if your interviewers can picture you in the uniform, and a pantsuit is a closer match. The same color and style guidelines apply: choose black, dark blue, or dark grey. A white or light colored blouse underneath is a good contrast; just don't go for anything too flashy. The blouse should not have jewels, sequins, or be made of reflective material. Think Sunday morning church rather than Friday night debauchery.

I get asked this question frequently: "I have a nice tan (insert non-traditional color of your choosing) suit that looks really good on me. Can I wear it?"

Black, dark blue, and dark grey (charcoal) are always safe bets. You'll never go wrong wearing a suit in one of these colors. Anything outside these basic colors and you're going out on a limb. If you're even asking the question, "Does this purple ensemble...?" my answer is no. Black, navy blue, or grey. Your interview is not the place to be fashionable. It is the place to be conservative and professional. That's what the company wants from their pilots.

Guys: don't get too creative with the shirt and tie combo either. I know it's more fun to express your individuality, but this isn't the time or place to do that. You can't go wrong with a white shirt.

The second most frequently asked question is: "I have a blue shirt and tie that look good together, Can I wear that?"

YOU CAN'T GO WRONG WITH A WHITE SHIRT. You can go wrong with something else.

Since you are wearing a dark suit and white shirt (RIGHT!?), a brightly colored tie with a conservative pattern creates a nice contrast. Consider going to a higher-end clothing store as opposed to the local Walmart. By brightly colored, I don't mean loud. It shouldn't have hula girls, airplanes, or Looney Tunes characters on it. It should not light up. Your tie should have nothing more than a conservative pattern on it. I know you're a unique pebble on the shore of the ocean, and you have a lucky tie your three-year old bought you that's never let you down, but DON'T succumb to those urges. Bright colors, conservative patterns. Stick to it.

"I'm interviewing at XYZ airlines, and I heard if you don't have a red tie on they won't hire you."

I've seen nice ties in all colors, and I don't put any stock in the belief that certain companies require certain color ties to be successful. Whatever you pick, just make sure it compliments your suit well and doesn't clash. The higher quality the tie, the better it will lie on your chest and not bunch up or wrinkle. This is a case where I wouldn't necessarily buy the cheapest tie I could find on the rack.

Is an expensive suit going to guarantee you the job? Not by itself, but it will pave the way. Remember how heavily first impressions weigh on your overall success. Start with the right momentum and it's easier to keep the interview going in the right direction. If you start out by stepping into a gigantic hole and breaking your ankle, it's hard to get the interview back on the right track.

Points to remember

- ✓ There are three suit colors you can never go wrong with: black, dark blue, or dark grey. Make sure the suit fits you well.
- ✓ Wear a white shirt with your suit. You cannot go wrong with a white shirt.
- ✓ Get a well-made tie that compliments your suit. The tie should have a conservative color pattern, nothing more.

Grooming

I was seated alone in a small room with an applicant. He was very personable, outgoing, and seemed to have everything together. We were talking about his background, and while he was talking I kept hearing a clicking sound. I tried to ignore it, but the more I tried the louder and more frequent it seemed to become until I was having a hard time following what the applicant was saying.

The applicant was done with his answer, so I had to ask because I thought maybe I was going crazy, "Do you hear a clicking sound in here?"

"Oh, yeah, it's probably this," he said, and then stuck his tongue out to reveal a huge barbell sticking through the middle of it.

"Ah...I see," I said as my tongue started throbbing just from looking at it. "So, you wear that all the time then?"

"Yeah, I can't really take it out or it will close up. Did you know your tongue is the fastest healing organ in your body?"

"I was not aware of that," I replied with complete sincerity.

Grooming is a more inclusive topic nowadays than simply getting a decent haircut and putting on some deodorant. Getting a haircut is part of it, don't get me wrong, but so is the jewelry you're wearing, cologne/perfume level, nail condition, amount of hair product and spikiness level, etc.

Here's the big picture: this is a professional-level job you're interviewing for, and you need to look the part. Imagine this situation: you're standing around the gate with your family waiting to board an aircraft. You notice one of the pilots walking past the gate to board the plane. He has a neck tattoo, 2" gauge earrings, flames running down the sides of his sunglasses, and he's chugging a Red Bull. Would you feel comfortable with that, or would you consider buying a ticket on a different airline next time (if not this time)? What type of expectation is that look setting? Is this going to be an uneventful airline flight or an *extreme* airline flight? No one wants an "extreme" flight on an airline. Absolutely no one, myself included. You need to look safe, dependable, and capable, not like you're only doing this pilot thing while you take a break from BASE jumping in your wingsuit.

Hair

For some of you guys out there, I know the easiest thing to do is head into the bathroom and use a set of Wahl clippers to give yourself a semi-acceptable haircut. Open up the purse strings, Ebenezer, and fork out a few shillings to get a *professional* haircut. You may not believe it, but there is actually a difference between a home haircut and one done in a salon. Don't go crazy with the styling, either. In terms of hairstyle, you should look like you just stepped out of a 1950s movie instead of the X games. Once you're off probation you can push the limits of the approved grooming standards, but for now shave off your soul patch and tone down the spiky hair. Hair should be cut and trimmed neatly above the collar of your interview shirt and sideburns should not extend past your ears.

For ladies, wear your hair in a conservative, professional style. Up or back generally sends the most professional impression. If your hair is too short for either of those, just make sure it's not hanging in your face. Think of something that would be appropriate for going to church with your grandmother. If you have any color in your hair that isn't normally found in nature, give yourself enough time to get it removed. On the makeup front, go easy and very conservative. When you're deciding how much to wear, repeat the phrase to yourself "less is more."

Nails

Check your hands and fingernails a few days before your interview. I'm not a big manicure guy personally, but I know men and women who get one before an interview, and I don't think it's a bad idea. Handshakes are a *big* part of the interview process (much more on that soon), and you're going to be offering your hand to multiple people throughout the day. Your hands should look presentable. Whether you decide to get a manicure or not, make sure your nails are trimmed and your hands are clean. You'll want to put off changing the oil in your car until the interview is over.

Ladies should not wear nail polish except for clear, or at *most* a very muted color. The best way to go with nails for an interview is a simple French tip; there's no way to go wrong with that. Your nails should also be of reasonable length. What's reasonable? If you can't shake someone's hand without raking them with your fingernails, they're too long. If your nails are starting to curve, they're too long. If you're asking yourself right now, "I wonder if my nails are too long?" they're too long. Painted designs, stickers, and small jewels are *never* OK for an interview. The operative word in that previous sentence is: *never.*

Fragrance

You want to be very judicious in your use of cologne or perfume on interview day. If you're in the middle of the simulator evaluation and the instructor inconspicuously dons the oxygen mask, you've overdone it. Many people don't like fragrance, and some people are flat out allergic to it. I've conducted interviews with people where I literally felt like I was suffocating because the applicant was wearing so much cologne. Deodorant or antiperspirant should be enough. Lay off the heavy stuff; too much can make people uncomfortable.

Tattoos and jewelry

That tattoo running all the way down your arm to your fingertips looks really cool on rock stars, but it gives a different impression when it's poking out of your interview suit. *Never* ok. Same thing with gauge earrings, nose rings, eyebrow rings, or anything else that looks like it may have come out of a tackle box and is now hanging in your facial area. Operative word: *never*. If you've already gotten that neck tattoo or stretched your earlobes out to unnatural proportions, you've come to this book too late. These choices are what I consider "career limiting," and you're going to have to look at some type of correction if you really want to make it somewhere in this field.

For men, jewelry should be limited to a professional looking watch and wedding band, if applicable. I know some guys like to wear their class rings, academy rings, etc., but I personally like the less is more philosophy. What's a professional watch? It should have hands, and its size should *not* lead to the discussion, "When does a watch become a wall clock?"

For ladies, the same goes for the watch and wedding band. Conservative earrings are acceptable. Just pick something that is basically a stud and doesn't dangle below your earlobe. Dangly bracelets are best left at home.

Points to remember

- ✓ For men, get a professional haircut a few days before your interview. Ladies should wear their hair in a conservative fashion.
- ✓ Trim your nails and make sure your hands are clean and presentable. They will be doing a lot of greeting on interview day.
- ✓ Don't gas out your interviewers. Leave the cologne or perfume at home.
- ✓ Visible tattoos aren't considered a good thing; same with any kind of "atypical" piercing.
- ✓ With jewelry: less is more.

Interview action figure: accessories included

If you don't already have one, you'll want to consider purchasing some type of briefcase. I've seen people show up for their interview carrying nothing but a stack of paperwork and their logbooks. Appearing like a homeless person staggering in off the street clutching papers to their chest isn't really the look you want to go for.

I've got the standard black leather rectangular case, and I've always been happy with it. I feel a little like Jimmy Stewart trapped in a 1950s-black-and-white-film when I'm carrying it, but it works. *Don't* bring a backpack. *Don't* dump everything out of your flight bag and use it as a briefcase substitute. *Don't* bring your entire pile of luggage and ask the receptionist if you can leave it behind the desk. Get some type of professional business case or satchel and bring *only* that.

I've seen more than one person cruise through with a metal aluminum briefcase. I wouldn't consider it unacceptable, but when it's combined with a dark suit ensemble it comes off looking a little secret agent-ish. I would recommend something dark and made from the skin of a cow for your interview case. Notice, I didn't say alligator, and I wouldn't mention it if I hadn't seen it happen. If you suck it up and get something nice, you'll get more use out of it than you may think over the years to come.

Three other items I never go to an interview without (in addition to what they ask you to bring):

1. Pen
2. Notepad
3. Breath mints

You're going to need to sign paperwork or write something down. It's nice to have your own pen rather than borrowing your interviewer's and writing a note on the gum wrapper in your pocket.

Breath mints are a very handy item to have on hand. You're going to be interacting with people in close quarters all day. If your breath smells like you just licked the inside of a toilet bowl, people won't enjoy meeting you as much as you may think. If you're participating in an all-day interview, you'll most likely break for lunch or a snack at some point. It's nice to pop in a breath mint and get ready for round two after your onion sandwich with extra garlic sauce.

Interview days can be long. I personally don't do well if I don't eat anything all day. My mood changes to Oscar The Grouch with a bad hangover and an ingrown toenail (or so I've been told). It's very difficult to perform at your peak if there's no fuel in the tank. I recommend sticking a PowerBar, Snickers bar, banana, etc. in your briefcase, just in case you need a little energy before your next event. If you opt for the banana, make sure you take it out of your briefcase following the interview, otherwise when you open it two years later you'll be buying a new briefcase.

There is one thing you need to check anytime you stop and eat during the interview process: make sure you don't have something stuck in your teeth. I interviewed a guy once with a gigantic black something or other stuck right between his two front teeth. I kept trying not to look at it. I kept trying not to think about it. After a while though, it was the only thing I could see while he was talking. Glance in a mirror before you present yourself for the job and make sure you're not carrying part of your breakfast along for the ride.

While it's not really an accessory, you're going to be bringing whatever you ate the night before with you to the interview. Just because Roscoe's Extra Hot Chili Joint is the only place within walking distance of your hotel doesn't mean that's the best place for you to eat.

If you have any type of digestive issues, make sure you account for that the night before and the morning of your interview. A lack of good planning can be...uncomfortable for everyone.

Points to remember

- ✓ Get a professional business briefcase for your interview. Bring a pen, notepad, and breath mints with you. Consider bringing a snack if the interview process will take all day.
- ✓ Don't eat or drink anything that may not agree with you the night before or the morning of your interview. Check your teeth before you walk into the building and make sure there's nothing stuck in them.

Don't use cheap gimmicks

I want to take a minute to mention gimmicks. What's a gimmick? I had one client I was prepping for an interview who wanted to put a paper cover over his logbook with "Go XYZ airlines!" type captions all over it. I'm not sure what he was trying to accomplish, but the idea reminded me of 6th grade math class where the girl I sat next to had "I Love Brad!" written all over her textbook in different colors.

I had another guy who wanted to wear an "XYZ airlines" baseball cap to the interview. When asked why he felt like he needed to wear a baseball cap, he said he wanted to reinforce how much he wanted the job and make sure they remembered him. I told him the fact that he was showing up to the interview proved he wanted the job, and being remembered as *the only* guy to ever show up to the interview in a baseball cap wasn't the type of memory you wanted to leave them with.

I've heard many similar ideas over the years, and believe me when I tell you these are two of the "better" ones. If you know how to give a strong interview performance, you don't need a cheap gag to stand out from the crowd. This book will give you the tools to give a strong performance. You don't need anything else.

I can tell you without hesitation that by and large the majority of interviews are uneventful and forgettable: John Doe completes the entire process, does a pretty good job. You fill out the paperwork giving him thumbs up and head home. A week later if someone asked you how John Doe's interview went, you probably won't remember unless something memorable happened. And by memorable I mean usually something bad (for the applicant). I can't *specifically* remember the majority of good applicants I've interviewed because everything goes like it should. Unless the applicant was way above average for some reason, most of these fade into the background. The train wrecks, oddballs, and comic relief, however, are always easy to remember.

When interviewers are meeting together after the fact, you don't want to be the subject of this conversation:

"You'll never guess what this person did in the interview," or "Check out the cover on this guy's logbook," or even, "Did you see the guy in the baseball cap?"

Almost all of these discussions end up in the decision that this person is outside the parameters the company is looking for.

Bottom line: if you're considering trying a stunt to make yourself memorable, I would strongly advise against it. There are a number of companies out there right now that have a reputation for wanting outgoing, energetic, unique individuals. I know of people coming up with zany schemes to try to make a point of how unique and fun they are. Big foam hats, cowboy boots with the interview suit, and on and on it goes. You can get those traits across in your interview presenting yourself effectively better than you can by trying to come up with some type of visual gag. You will get the job using your verbal and non-verbal skills, not props.

Points to remember

✓ Don't use a gimmick to try to draw attention. That's not the kind of attention you want.

Leave your toys at home

One of my favorite fictional characters in print (and later on screen) once said, "The things you own end up owning you." That statement has never been more relevant than it is right now in our gadget-based society. Don't let all the junk we feel compelled to drag around on a daily basis affect the course of your career, because it truly can.

Interview Train Wreck #7

This wasn't an experience I personally witnessed, but happened to a good friend of mine.

This person had a respectable amount of experience, enough to be competitive for any job out there. He scored an interview with a company that was based in his hometown (he was currently doing a long commute), and was a step up in pay and equipment. The new job could potentially improve his quality of life by, oh, somewhere around 1000%. He wanted it badly, and asked me to help him practice about a week prior to the interview.

I did an interview prep session with him. His technical knowledge was very solid, and his main concern focused on the Human Resource side of the interview.

I started out with my normal spiel, talking about dress code and body language.

"Yeah, yeah, I know all that," he said. "Let's just go over the HR questions."

"This stuff is just as important as answering questions, but hey, it's your nickel," I replied. "If you want to move on we can, but I'd recommend going over it."

"Just ask me some questions," he stated confidently.

"OK," I said. Trying to sum all the intricacies of good interview presentation into one short statement, I added, "Make sure your suit looks good, shut off your cell phone, give a firm handshake and make good eye contact. Be friendly and outgoing. Moving on…"

So that's what we did. He had some rough spots on the HR side but I felt like we got everything ironed out pretty well. I was confident he would do well. I asked him to call me as soon as he was done and let me know how it went.

A couple of days went by, and my phone rang. It was him, and I asked him how the interview had gone.

"Not very well," he said.

I was surprised, "OK. Give me the scoop."

I was worried he had a problem with some of the issues we'd gone over during the prep.

Nothing is ever that simple. As it turns out, he was running late for the interview because he had difficulty finding the building. He walked through the door just in the nick of time. They called him back for a 2 on 1 interview: 1 instructor pilot and 1 HR rep.

They had just sat down and finished introductions when his cell phone rang. Loudly rang. I think he had the ringer set to level 11 (out of 10). Did I mention the ringer was a song called "Down with the Sickness?" If you're not familiar with that particular melody, imagine a guy screaming "COME ON, GET DOWN WITH THE SICKNESS!!!" into the microphone as loudly as he possibly can while being accompanied by driving heavy metal guitar riffs.

My friend reached down and silenced the ringer as quickly as physics would allow, but not before everyone in the room got a good flavor for "Down with the Sickness."

The voicemail notification sounded loudly a few seconds later, and he was forced to take his attention away from the interview as he powered down his phone.

The pilot interviewer seemed slightly amused. He had kind of a half-smile on his face, but began quickly writing something that I would guess wasn't good. The HR lady, however, looked at my friend like he'd just skinned a newborn baby and eaten it right in front of them.

My friend tried to lighten the mood, and made some comment like, "I guess that doesn't look very good."

The HR lady replied, with no smile whatsoever, "No, it doesn't."

The instructor pilot asked his questions and took about 20 minutes.

When it was the HR lady's turn, she only asked one question.

"Why do you want to come to airline X?"

That was it.

About a week later, he got a letter saying thanks but you're not a good fit for our company. It was unfortunate, since he and his entire family really wanted this job. This is an important example of how one tiny thing, forgetting to turn off your cell phone, can have serious consequences. Expensive lesson for him.

The phone call, incidentally, was from his wife. She assumed the call would go right to voicemail and wanted to wish him luck.

I couldn't make this stuff up if I tried.

I had similar experiences to the one above when I was giving the welcome brief to a room full of applicants. Somewhere in the neighborhood of once a month, a cell phone would go off while I was addressing the interview group. I'll tell you from personal experience that when you're talking in front of a bunch of people and a phone starts ringing, it's annoying. I always knew whose phone it was that was ringing, because they were the one frantically trying to silence it. Not a good start to your interview.

No one likes being without our electronic umbilical cords. How will you Twitter all your friends about your interview without it, or update your real-time Facebook status to "in interview?" The world will just have to wait, the old-fashioned way, but believe me it will keep spinning for the whole day you have to go through this process.

I recommend leaving your phone in the car. Just... leave it. You can have every good intention of shutting if off for the interview. You can tie a string around your finger that morning so you don't forget. You can remind yourself *again* that you need to shut it off as you walk in the building. Then things start happening fast. You're meeting people, you're going here, you're going there, and the next thing you know your phone is playing, "*Down with the Sickness*" for your interviewers and they ask you why there's a string on your finger. It's much easier to... just... leave... it.

If you don't have a place to leave it, or there's information on it you need for the interview, make *absolutely sure* you shut off the phone. Put your watch on the other arm as a reminder; tape the phone to your head; just do whatever it takes to remind yourself to shut it off. Point of clarification (because I know someone is wondering about just setting it to vibrate): *Setting your phone to vibrate is not the same as shutting it off.* A phone vibrating in a small room with three or four people sitting around a table is just the same as ringing, except that you sit there and pretend it's not really ringing, even though everyone in the room knows it is. Just shut it off, or better yet... LEAVE IT somewhere that's not your interview.

I know listening to an iPod is the pastime of choice, and it's hard to go a whole day without singing along to a Lady Gaga song, but leave that at home as well. There's a lot of waiting on interview day. You wait for your interview. You wait for the sim. You wait while your logbooks are reviewed. That's a lot of waiting, and you're just going to have to deal with it.

An interviewer I worked with came into the lobby to bring an applicant back for his interview a couple of years ago. The interviewer announced the name, but no one responded. He said it again, but no one responded. He looked at the name again thinking he was butchering it so badly its owner couldn't recognize it, but it was pretty straightforward, like John Smith. Looking around, he saw one (younger) guy with his back to him and a set of ear buds in his ears, looking out the window. He went over and tapped him on the shoulder. The applicant turned around and took the ear buds out. Sure enough he was the guy. That's a good way to annoy your interviewer right out of the gate.

Always keep in mind where you are and why you're there. You're there to convince this company that employing you for (potentially) the next few decades is the best decision they can make. Don't let inappropriate use of electronic gadgets affect their decision.

Points to remember

✓ Leave your electronics somewhere else during the interview. If you can't leave your phone for whatever reason, make absolutely sure it is off before you walk in the building. Vibrate is not off.

Part 3

Actions speak louder than words

Having the right appearance is critical to making the first impression, and a good first impression gets the momentum going in the right direction. With that being said, we're running a marathon here, not a sprint. A good first impression can only get you so far. Your interviewers might like your outward appearance, but if you display the social tact of a primate, the end result won't be positive.

Depending on whom you listen to, as much as 93% of human communication is non-verbal. What does that mean to you? It means you can say one thing verbally, but your actions may be saying something altogether different. Since so much of communication is non-verbal, and interviewers are trained *specifically* to interpret it, you need to have a good sense of the non-verbal messages you're sending.

You can say out loud, "I'm the best pilot you could possibly hope to hire; this company will be stronger by my being a part of it."

You can (and maybe should) even believe that. But, if you're saying that quietly to your shoulder as you avoid meeting your interviewer's eyes and bounce your leg nervously up and down, they're probably not going to buy it.

Whether you know it yet or not, you're going to be doing a lot of non-verbal communication with your interviewers. A tremendous amount, in fact, and they are going to be observing you like a hawk eyeing up a mouse for dinner. Any disagreement between the words coming out of your mouth and the message your body language is sending can create a question in their mind. That is what you don't want. Your body language determines if you appear outgoing, introverted, confident, unsure, aggressive, submissive, friendly, distant, just plain old weird, and a million variations in between.

This is the image you want to project: calm, capable, and friendly. We're going to focus on what actions send those messages. You want to steer away from actions that may send the impression you're an introverted sociopath who's unsure of himself, but thank you for coming today Mr. John Wayne Gacy.

Here's the million dollar secret to having effective body language: you have to demonstrate it consistently, without having to think about it all the time. That means you have to start practicing it all the time, starting today.

When you took your first check-ride to get your instrument rating did you simply read a book on instrument flying, and then go hop in the airplane and perform? Probably not. You spent a lot of time *practicing*. When you got to a certain proficiency level, *then* you took the check ride. Interviewing effectively is a skill, just like flying. If you don't practice beforehand, on interview day you're just throwing a dart at a board and hoping you'll get a bull's-eye. I can tell you from experience, without practice you probably won't.

You need to practice, critique, and improve to consistently perform well. Practicing body language and presentation is just as important as practicing answering questions. You can use a mirror, a video recorder, or your smart phone, but you *need* to get a third-person perspective on how you look when you're standing, sitting, greeting, and answering. Record yourself as you work through a set of questions, and then watch it afterward. You'll find that when you're focused on answering questions, and not on consciously maintaining your presentation, your natural tendencies present themselves. You can't fix something if you don't know what's broken, so watch yourself carefully. Once you're aware of the fact that you stick your finger in your ear every time you're contemplating something, it's easy to stop.

From the "True Story" files... and I know this one is true because it happened to me. I wasn't always good at being interviewed. In fact, I only became good (and maybe even slightly obsessive about it) because my first one went so poorly. In hindsight, it was a positive experience because it shaped how I approached every interview after that. It didn't seem at all positive at the time, however, it just really sucked.

Interview Train Wreck #8

I was interviewing for an internship with United Airlines. That may not seem like a big deal, at first. Who cares about an unpaid internship, right? The value of the internship, however, was that upon completing it you had a guaranteed interview for a pilot slot (once you met their minimums). United Airlines was THE number one airline to work for at the time. It was incredibly hard to get an interview there unless you were (literally) an astronaut, had 10s of thousands of hours, or were heavily connected. This internship was literally worth its weight in gold. The interview was the same one pilot applicants got minus the simulator evaluation, and just getting it was highly competitive. Somehow I slipped through the cracks and got one scheduled.

I remember giving this interview process zero forethought. Absolutely zero. I don't know what I thought they were going to ask me when I walked in there.

I guess I figured it would be along the lines of: "Hey Rick, we've been waiting for you! When can you start?"

Instead, I wandered in wearing my slightly mismatched suit (The Black Suit!), and surprisingly they started asking questions. Hard questions. Hard questions about flying stuff that I wasn't ready for. Thirty seconds into the interview, I realized: I AM NOT PREPARED FOR THIS. You may not know what that feels like, sitting in an interview chair watching a great opportunity slip away right before your eyes. Believe me when I say you don't ever want to know.

My level of discomfort grew (as I was fumbling around with answers that didn't really answer their questions), and I realized I was talking to my hands instead of the people asking the questions. I heard a squeaking sound repeating over and over again. It took a few minutes before I realized it was the swivel chair I was sitting in and apparently swinging back and forth, which was making the noise. I could go on and on, but I think you probably smell what I'm stepping in.

Big picture: this was a train wreck for a lot of different reasons, first and foremost being lack of preparation. What I was most disappointed in about myself though was how I acted in that interview chair. It could have been a case study for how NOT to present oneself.

You can give a wrong answer in an interview. You can give a subjective answer your interviewers might not necessarily agree with (more on that later). If you are giving a great personal presentation, that can make up for a lot. An awful lot. Remember, the entire process is subjective. You can make mistakes, as long as the total package you're selling is solid, and still get the job. Or, you can make *no mistakes*, come off like a jerk, and not get the job. Let's talk now about how to make sure you're sending the *right* message non-verbally.

Handshakes go a long way

I'm going to warn you right now, bad handshakes are my pet peeve. If you can't figure out how to give a good handshake, you won't get far in life.

Interview Train Wreck #9

I came out to meet and greet an applicant face to face after reviewing his paperwork for the interview. His application package was great. He had all the documentation we'd requested and it was all filled out correctly. Always a good start. It appeared things would go swimmingly.

I put my hand out to shake his, and what he offered in response was a cold, limp, dead fish handshake. It was like grabbing something that crawled out of a grave.

That's it. The whole enchilada. I can't remember anything else about his interview except for that pathetic handshake.

The interview was over in the first 3 seconds of meeting. All I could think about for the next hour was that I couldn't wait to go wash my hand because it felt dirty somehow.

This is my absolute pet peeve, not just in an interview setting, but in any social or professional setting in the world. There is nothing that sends a worse impression than a limp handshake. It doesn't matter if it's a man, a woman, or a hobbit.

I've spoken to many people in recruiting both inside and outside of aviation. The general consensus is that anyone who can't muster enough enthusiasm to actually grip your hand the first time they meet you is an employment risk not worth taking. If you are a limp handshake offender, I'm going to ask you to do the world a favor right now and cut your hands off to spare the rest of us this repeated indignity.

If you find yourself interviewing for a job you really DON'T want for some reason, give a weak, limp handshake and the rest will take care of itself.

I tried to put none too fine a point on the value I place on a handshake. I would even go so far as to say nearly everyone in any level of hiring feels the same way. If you don't give a good handshake, you don't send a good impression. Period, dot, end of statement.

So what constitutes a good handshake? First, let's talk about position. Square your shoulders to the person you're meeting and hold your hand out straight in front of you with your thumb pointed at the ceiling. DO NOT twist your body as you offer your hand, resulting in one shoulder being ahead of the other. That implies informality. DO NOT turn your hand sideways. Offering a handshake with the back of your hand toward the ceiling implies dominance. Offering your hand with the palm up implies submissiveness. Offering a closed fist and saying, "Hit it" implies you're going to have a short interview. Square shoulders, open hand, thumb up is the goal. Don't get creative.

Three grip levels are available to you: limp, bone crusher, and normal. My recommendation is to apply the normal grip level. A limp handshake is one where the hand dangles lifelessly and no pressure is applied during the handshake process. A limp handshake implies submissiveness, lack of confidence, and general un-enthusiasm. A bone crusher, on the other hand, is when the applicant tries to quantify his/her desire for the job through the strength of their grip. This can come across as trying to physically dominate your interviewer. Again, not the impression you're going for.

A normal handshake grip is similar to what you would use to carry an umbrella or your briefcase. The web of your hand (the area between your thumb and forefinger) should meet the web of your interviewer's. Apply your grip to the interviewer's hand itself, don't just grab their fingers or use only your thumb to apply pressure. Release the handshake before the end of your interviewer's introduction; usually about 1-3 pumps if you need a number.

If your hands tend to be cold, put them in your pocket to warm them up prior to the introduction. If you have clammy hands, casually wipe your palm against your pant leg or skirt as you raise your hand so you can offer a dry, warm hand for the shaking.

Grab a friend or family member and practice your handshake a couple of times. If you see them wincing in pain or they snatch their hand back and cradle it in terror, you'll want to adjust your technique. Eventually, you'll get to the point where you're comfortable giving a consistently good handshake, and you can move on to bigger and better things.

Points to remember

✓ A handshake can make or break your interview. When giving a handshake, square your shoulders and put your hand straight in front of you with your thumb pointed to the ceiling. Apply a normal grip level throughout the handshake. 1-3 pumps are sufficient.

Conversational speaking

When nervous, people sometimes have a tendency to talk louder and faster than normal. If their confidence is lacking, they have a tendency to talk quieter. Developing normal conversational skills in a stressful interview environment is actually a skill set by itself.

The first thing you can start working on is talking in a smooth and even tone.

If you haven't listened to yourself on tape recently, you may immediately notice a lot of ums, ahs, pauses, or "filler" words and statements. Try to phase these words out of your statements.

You'll want to avoid common repetitive colloquialisms that seem to creep into our daily language. For example:

Ending each statement with something similar to, "…ya know?"

Interjecting the word "like" into every sentence, "…like…and then…like…"

Using the words "totally," "awesome," or the dreaded "Totally Awesome!" combination.

You also want to avoid using any type of slang:

"I want to leave my present company because it's an epic fail and they're always jerking me around with my schedule."

I know twerking and sexting and many other pop culture words have been added to the dictionary recently, but it's best to avoid slang altogether. Here's an easy rule to follow: if you're not positive your grandparents would understand the meaning of a particular word (in context), don't use it.

You've probably guessed just from what you've read so far that I struggle with slang issues myself, but I can turn it off for half a day to do an interview. Fo shizzle.

Whether you're giving a complex answer or greeting someone for the first time, let your statements flow smoothly instead of breaking them up and interjecting words and phrases from the examples above. The net result can be an unprofessional image.

When you're watching yourself on video, be on the lookout for nervous movements or fidgeting. Work on consciously weeding out these actions during your practice sessions. Nervous habits come out when you least expect them *and* you're under stress, such as when you're thinking hard on an answer. Sit in a chair with your feet flat on the floor while you practice your answers. Put your back against the chair and sit up straight. Don't slouch or lean.

You'll be meeting and greeting a lot on interview day. When you are introduced or greeted by someone, square your shoulders to the person you're meeting and stand up straight. Once you've observed interview events enough, you can almost instantly pick out applicants who are going to do well just by how they stand. You're going for friendly and confident. You can't pull that off if you're subconsciously shrinking away from people every time you meet with them.

As you advance through the process, you'll eventually interact with people while seated. Sit like you stand, straight up with shoulders slightly back, squarely facing the people with whom you're interacting. Do not lean forward in your chair or slouch back. Both of these actions have negative associations. Keep your feet flat on the floor and avoid fidgeting, bouncing a leg, swinging your knees back and forth, or any other repetitive movements. Crossing your leg and placing an ankle on your knee while seated is considered a very defensive and guarded position. The same goes for crossing your arms in front of your chest. If these are positions you typically sit in and find comfortable, you'll want to avoid them. Keep both feet flat on the floor at all times, except when you're walking.

Hand gestures

I'm not talking about flipping someone the bird, although I would also advise against that in your interview. Some people have a tendency to talk with their hands. I, myself, fall into this category. Gesturing with your hands *slightly* while you speak isn't necessarily a bad thing, just don't get too animated or it starts to detract from your performance. Imagine there is a one-foot by one-foot box in front of you. If you use your hands a lot when you talk, keep them in this box. Any hand movements outside the 1x1 box and it can affect your credibility.

You'll generally want to fold your hands and put them in your lap while seated. I put them in my lap because if I place them on the table, I have a tendency to clench them together and hunch forward, which can send an overly aggressive impression.

One unconscious mannerism that signals deception is when a person touches their face, ear, or nose while speaking to you. Adhere to the 1x1 box rule, and you won't have a problem. Under no circumstances should you raise your hands above shoulder level *at any point* during the interview, unless your hair has actually caught on fire.

A hand gesture that conveys openness and honesty is showing your palms while speaking. If you gesture with your hands, position your palms up whenever possible. Avoid pointing directly at someone, and avoid clenching your hands into fists while speaking or listening.

Respect personal space

Here's a big scientific word: Proxemics. That's a fancy-schmancy word for the study of measurable distances between people when they meet. I like to dumb things down to my level whenever possible, so I just call it the personal space bubble. Everyone maintains a certain bubble of space around himself or herself that they consider theirs. Your cultural upbringing, the setting you're in, and the participants involved generally dictate the size of that bubble. In North America and Europe, one's personal space bubble is about 1.5 feet around them. People raised in these cultures reserve anything inside that 1.5-foot bubble for intimate acquaintances. Unless you've done *serious* interview preparation, you won't be on intimate terms with your interviewers. If you are, my hat goes off to you.

In the interview setting, when you're meeting and greeting, you want to be about 2 to 4 feet from the person or people you're interacting with. Anything inside that 2-foot bubble and you'll give the impression of being a "close talker." You run the risk of making your interviewer uncomfortable, and that's not a good way to start the day.

I've dealt with close talking offenders during interviews and as interview prep clients. With the clients, we discussed why they felt the distance they chose for interaction was appropriate. Many times it's simply a cultural difference. The perception of personal space in India, for example, is much closer than we are used to in the US. In Japan, Americans can be viewed as distant and standoffish because of the physical distance they maintain during interaction, while Americans sometimes view Japanese as being too familiar. No one is intentionally trying to be offensive, but the difference in the perception of acceptable personal space can create a negative impression.

I worked with one guy in particular who was from India. He had previously been unsuccessful in two separate interviews. When we met for the first time and shook hands...boom...he was literally so close I could count the pores on his nose. We worked through that and a few other issues, most of them culturally related. His interview following our work together was successful.

Culture isn't always a factor. Sometimes an applicant feels like closer proximity equates to being friendlier. You need to give the impression you're friendly, so closer is better right? That is true up to a point. Like all things in life, the middle way is generally the best way. You don't want to get right up in your interviewer's face, but at the same time you can't have a normal conversation with someone from eight feet away. That can imply you're trying not to catch something from them. Remember, 2 to 4 feet is the sweet spot.

If you're having a hard time consistently judging the distance to stand from someone, especially when it's a departure from how you've grown up, try this:

Use a piece of tape to make a mark on the floor 2 feet from a mirror. Practice walking up to the mirror and saying hello. Do this several times over a couple of days. You'll get a good feel for the right distance to stand without invading someone's personal space or acting like you're being introduced to a plague carrier.

Points to remember

✓ You should maintain a 2- 4 foot distance from people you meet and interact with for your interview.

Eye contact

Eye contact ranks right up there with the initial handshake in terms of importance. The handshake sends an instantaneous first impression. Think of eye contact as a handshake that occurs over a much longer period of time. If a handshake is like a sprint, then eye contact is a marathon, and you must maintain your pace for the entire interview. Eye contact is where people new to interviewing have the most trouble. A lack of eye contact can affect your credibility, result in failure to establish any type of rapport with your interviewers, and leave them generally ambivalent about bringing you onboard.

Looking a person in the eyes acknowledges your interest and involvement in the conversation. Maintaining good eye contact also demonstrates your self-confidence and honesty. Prolonged, uninterrupted eye contact can be construed as a sign of aggression, which is why in normal conversation we break eye contact momentarily and then re-establish it. If you have a tendency to stare at people unblinking for long periods of time, you may come off a bit like Hannibal Lecter.

Looking back again to my own personal interview train wreck, I had an issue with eye contact, stemming from the fact that I was insecure because I had done nothing to get ready for the interview. I had nothing to be confident about. I was unsure of both my knowledge level and capabilities, and that was made clear by my eye contact, or lack thereof. Looking down, I was talking to my hands, and talking to my shoes. I was having a conversation with the side of the room where no one was sitting. Basically, it was the worst performance you can imagine. Having given such a poor performance previously, the stress started mounting when my next interview rolled around.

"What if this one goes just as poorly? Maybe I'm not cut out for this. I spent all this time and money to be a pilot and I'm never going to make it. Where's the number for that truck driving school?"

All those negative thoughts going through your head will come out in your body language, specifically your eye contact, if you're not careful. How do you prevent this from happening? Just being aware of what you're doing with your eye contact is the first thing. Building confidence and establishing habit patterns is the next. Practicing everything we've been going over is the last piece of the puzzle, which we'll get to shortly.

Maintaining eye contact with someone during conversation is a standard common courtesy. The interview process isn't your standard conversation, however. There's a strong chance, depending on the company, that more than one person will interview you simultaneously. There will be times you will need to pause and think through your answers, and times you may be stumped on an answer. This is when being aware of what's going on with your eye contact becomes important.

When there's more than one person in the room firing questions at you, we refer to it as a panel interview, and eye contact can be challenging under these conditions. In a panel interview setting there is a tendency to only look at and answer the interviewer asking the question. You need to include everyone in the room in all of your answers. Shift your eye contact from one interviewer to the next throughout your answer. Even when they're not looking at you (they may be looking down or writing something), keep attempting to establish eye contact with everyone. The only exception to this rule is for short answers to technical questions. If you are asked a question whose answer only consists of a few words, it's acceptable to maintain eye contact with only the interviewer posing the question.

As you're answering questions and maintaining eye contact, at some point you'll be asked something that requires some contemplation. Where should you look while you're thinking? Anytime there's a pause and you have to think, try to look up. Looking up gives the impression you're being genuine and truthful. Looking down gives the impression you're being evasive and deceitful. In the vast majority of interviews I've done, I would eventually ask a question about something in the applicant's past they weren't proud of: a check ride failure, speeding ticket, animal molestation, whatever. I wasn't trying to make them feel uncomfortable, but it was something we had to go over and document. Every time someone told a story and had a hard time maintaining eye contact, I got the impression they were not being completely honest. Constantly shifting your eyes around the room sends an impression of being nervous or evasive.

Here's a good example: Have you ever seen a child get in trouble for misbehaving? The next time you have the opportunity to witness it, or if you just want to run out and start yelling at some random kid in the street, pay careful attention to their eyes.

I walked into the bathroom not too long ago and found my son giving the dog a bath in the toilet. SIGH. This was a recurring issue. I know that *he knows* that dogs don't go in toilets, unless maybe they're on fire, but that's another story altogether. I told him, "No," and asked him why he was giving the dog a bath in the toilet. Again. He then produced a long and extremely detailed narrative. It involved the dog actually telling him she needed a bath in the toilet. Guess where he looked the entire time he told the story. He looked down at the floor, then over at the corner, then back at the floor. He looked everywhere he could to not meet my eyes.

Grownups can have a tendency to do the exact same thing. Being nervous can easily make you revert to this behavior. Believe me when I say if you're interviewing for a job you really want, the butterflies will be fluttering and you'll be nervous. If you're nervous and shifting your gaze around constantly, it may give the impression of not being truthful, when in reality you are.

Points to remember

✓ Maintain steady eye contact with everyone in the room at all times, even if they're not maintaining eye contact with you. When you have to think, look up and then come back to maintaining eye contact with your interviewers.

Smiles are free

If you're interviewing for a job, you should look like you're glad to be there instead of like you're fulfilling court-ordered community service. An easy way to act friendly and upbeat is by smiling. If someone smiles at you while you're interacting, it leaves you with a positive impression. Smiling doesn't cost anything, and it can show your interviewers you're enjoyable to be around.

Interview Train Wreck #10

This interview was a train wreck on many levels. I thought a lot about which section it would apply to, and I put it here because the guy did not crack a smile at any point. I think that alone was the biggest problem with his performance, although there were many.

The whole situation started when I collected and reviewed this applicant's logbook. I introduced myself and stuck out my hand to shake his.

"Hi," he said giving a lame, very borderline handshake.

No smile. Not even a small grin. He had a look on his face like someone had just run over his dog.

And oh, how I hate lame handshakes. I may have mentioned that.

Three seconds into the interview and I'm already starting to build a case not to hire him, because frankly, I can tell almost instantaneously, that I don't want to be stuck on a trip with him for days. First impressions.

I asked if I could have his logbooks for review while he took the written test.

He didn't hand me his logbooks. Instead he jerked his head toward where they were stacked on the table.

Overall, he gave the vibe that he either was too good to be here or didn't want to be here at all. I decided I'd help him in his goal.

The song "Mr. Sunshine, bring me a dream..." started repeating over and over in my head as I went back to look through his logbooks, so I named him Mr. Sunshine.

I started reviewing his logbooks. They weren't terrible, but they weren't great either. He hadn't signed any logbook pages in the last year. As I looked more closely, it appeared he put his last year's worth of entries in for the interview by writing in monthly summaries of his time. See the logbook section for my take on monthly summaries of flight time.

Then, I got some answers. After looking through his application, I saw that he was recently furloughed. That explained some of his unhappiness. He'd spent his years at a commuter, built his time and gone to the majors, and was now back at the regional level again.

I could see how that would put someone in a bad mood. But a regional job was better than no job, so maybe he should be happy to have an opportunity instead of acting like it was an inconvenience. After thinking it over for a while I decided to give him the benefit of the doubt, try to forget my first impression, and start from scratch.

When he was done with the written test I returned his logbooks and said, "Here are your logbooks, thank you. We'll call you back for the interview in a few minutes. I just wanted to let you know there weren't any signatures on the last several pages of your logbook. You may want to take a look at that when you have a chance."

"That doesn't seem like a big deal," he replied, continuing to scowl and snatching the logbooks out of my hand. "The times are there, aren't they? That's what's important."

I heard that song again in my head, "Mr. Sunshine...bring me a dream..."

"Like I said, I just wanted to let you know so you could sign them if you wanted to."

I'm really not very hard to get along with. Really! All he had to do was say, "Sure, no problem," or "Whoops, my mistake," and I wouldn't have thought anything more about it. Instead, I was thinking about how I'd rather have my eyelids stapled open than spend a day in the cockpit with Mr. Sunshine, and that was after only exchanging a few sentences with him.

As I was gathering all the paperwork to bring him back for the interview, the head of the pilot-recruiting department, who we'll call Colletta, came into the room. Colletta asked who was interviewing John Doe (aka Mr. Sunshine).

Colletta is about 5 feet tall, white haired, and one of the nicest people you could ever meet. To this day she reminds me of Aunt Bea from the Andy Griffith Show. Every time we spoke I expected her to reach out, pinch my cheek, and ask me if I wanted some lemonade in her slightly southern accent.

I responded to her that I had Mr. Sunshine's paperwork and was going to be doing the interview.

"I just wanted to let you know this guy had been personally recommended by the VP of flight ops. He called me this morning," she informed me.

Awesome.

Maybe that explained why Mr. Sunshine acted like I was annoying him. He figured he already had the job and this was a formality.

I said, "Well, Colletta, there's a problem. I've spoken maybe twenty words to this guy and I can already tell you there's no way I'm recommending him."

I gave her the rundown on what had happened, and asked if she would sit in on the interview so I could hear what she thought. After all, maybe I was having a bad day and overreacting.

"Oh, and thanks for handing me the political hand grenade by the way," I added.

She giggled her Aunt Bea giggle as we went to meet the applicant.

We brought Mr. Sunshine back to the interview room where I introduced Mr. Sunshine to Colletta.

He gave her the same no-smile, "Hi" and lame handshake he'd given me, which made me feel better. At least it wasn't just me.

What ensued was one of the most surreal interview experiences I've ever had. He had no paperwork. Nothing. He hadn't made one copy of any of his documents, and hadn't filled out anything we'd sent him.

I asked him if he had any proof of his educational background whatsoever, because I needed to include something in his packet, even if it was unofficial transcripts or the credit-card-sized diploma some schools gave you.

"I graduated twenty years ago," he said. "I don't have any of that stuff."

Not, "I didn't have time to get it," or "I'll send it later," or even "I forgot it."

I pulled out some Jeppesen charts and asked him a few technical questions; instrument approach procedures, obstacle clearances, that kind of thing. Again, he acted annoyed by my questions. On top of acting annoyed and not smiling at all the entire time, he gave all the wrong answers.

He gave answers and gave them like he knew exactly what he was talking about, but he didn't. If you want to be a cocky ass, that's fine, but you'd better know your stuff. There's nothing worse than an a-hole who has no idea what he's talking about.

I was done. I didn't need to waste any more of Colletta's or my time. I didn't care if the King of Persia recommended this guy; I wasn't ever going to fly with him.

I was wrapping up everything when he reached into his bag, not a briefcase but an emptied-out flight bag (surprise). I couldn't imagine what he was reaching for, since he hadn't actually brought anything. He pulled something out of his case and flopped it onto the table. It was a Jeppesen Instrument Training Chart. The training chart is a study guide that gives definitions for all the symbols on the chart.

"Next time you do an interview, use this," he said. "It works a lot better."

I said that was all I had for him, thanks for coming.

Mr. Sunshine stood up, said he'd see us around, and left the room. He never smiled once during the entire interview.

He did a lot of things I didn't like during the interview, but it was the way he spoke and acted that was the worst. If he had said this stuff with a smile on his face, it would have come across totally different. Saying it the way he did, with a sullen, serious look the entire time, gave the worst impression I've ever seen.

I turned to Colletta and asked, "So what do you think?"

Colletta, the spitting image of the forever wholesome and nurturing Aunt Bea, looked me straight in the eye and said, "There's no f@#king way we're hiring that guy."

I think I blushed. I never knew Aunt Bea said the f-word.

A little personality goes a long way. As an interviewer, you can overlook a certain measure of technical deficiency or lack of experience if a person has the positive attitude and personality to make up for it. How do you show your interviewers you have a positive attitude and a good personality? Smile at them, as much as possible.

An applicant may not know this or that piece of aviation trivia. If they're happy, smiling, and upbeat throughout the interview that's what you remember, not the one or two questions they missed. I know we're all pilots here and everyone wants to be calm, cool, and collected under pressure, so you don't need to overdo it. You don't necessarily have to dance around on the table like a clown with a manic smile plastered on your face. You just need to project a friendly, positive attitude. Smiling comfortably while you're talking is an easy way to do that.

Try something the next time you're buying a coffee or checking out from a store: Ask the total stranger you're interacting with how their day is going with a very serious and intense look on your face. See how they answer. If you freak them out and they call for help, run away and never go back. Now, go to a *different* store and ask the same question with a big smile on your face. Compare the responses. I'll bet the person you talked to with a smile was much more forthcoming. That's because people like talking to other friendly people, and friendly people smile when they talk.

Being professional doesn't mean pretending you have the emotional range of a robot. You can be sharp, professional, friendly and outgoing all at the same time. And that is exactly how you want to act. A good way to send that impression is to use your smile. You don't need to look like The Joker, smile just enough so it looks like you're having an enjoyable time, and your interviewers will be inclined to respond in kind.

Here's another test: Look in the mirror and introduce yourself to yourself. Do it once with no emotion. Do it once with a smile on your face. Who would you rather fly with? When you're being introduced, have a big smile on your face. Smile while you're talking to your interviewers, and smile when you conclude your interview.

One question the interviewers are trying to answer is, "What is this person going to be like as an employee?"

The pilot side of the equation wants to see how being strapped into a cockpit with you for days on end will be. HR wants to know how you're going to interact with customers and other employees. Show them, by using your smile, that you're the type of person others will enjoy working with, instead of counting down the minutes until they can get away from you.

Points to remember

✓ Demonstrate and maintain a positive attitude over the entire course of your interview. An easy way to do this is by smiling at your interviewers whenever you can.

Mind your surroundings

You have to pay attention to where you are and what you're doing on interview day. Forgetting why you're there can have undesirable consequences.

The applicants for the day were milling around in the lobby talking amongst themselves in small groups. Everyone in the lobby was wearing a dark suit, white shirt interview combination. At the center of one particular group was a very animated gentleman speaking loudly to the gaggle surrounding him. Let's call him Loud Talker. Some individuals talk when they're nervous. The more nervous they get, the more they talk and the louder they talk. It's like a runway nuclear reaction feeding off itself. Loud Talker must have been extremely nervous because he was approaching critical mass.

The thing the applicants, and Loud Talker, didn't know was that one of the suits was occupied by our intern. He wasn't trying to be sneaky. He was just waiting by the receptionist desk to take everyone back to the briefing room at 9:00A.M., which he did every day.

As it turns out, Loud Talker and one of the other applicants in his group had worked at the same company. They began entertaining the other onlookers with their stories about said company.

As related by our intern:

Both Loud Talker and his buddy knew Chief Pilot Jones (not his real name).

Oh, what an a-hole Chief Pilot Jones was.

Loud Talker stormed into Chief Pilot Jones' office and quit on the spot, telling him to f&k off in the process (his exact words).*

Loud Talker's buddy thought that was fantastic and man did that a-hole deserve it (again, his exact words minus the hyphen).

What a wonderful time they were having reliving past glories which is fine, except for the fact that they were having this conversation on their interview day, in front of a member of the interview staff. The funny thing is that even after the intern identified himself and led them back to the briefing room, they were totally unaware he heard everything they'd been saying. In the interview world, we call that "being oblivious."

The intern put on a video in the briefing room, and then ran to tell us what he'd overheard. Ran.

As an interviewer, you're always on the lookout for anything that will be different, amusing, or at least memorable. Loud Talker was an opportunity for all three. Four of us were doing interviews that day and a battle ensued over who got him. Since I was the senior interviewer (and loudest whiner), I won. The next most senior interviewer got Loud Talker's buddy.

What is the fundamental problem here? Do I want to hire someone who quits by storming into the chief pilot's office and tells him to f&*k off? Nope. Would I hire someone who can't act professional and refrain from using profanity in a public place for two measly hours? Definitely not. What concerns me even more is hiring someone who's oblivious to his or her surroundings. That's a safety issue. Do you want to get on an airplane with someone who's so busy M-Fing everyone that he doesn't notice he's flying into a mountain? Absolutely not.

So I got Loud Talker in the interview and asked him about his job history. When Chief Pilot Jones' company came up, I asked him how he'd resigned.

He told me he gave them a letter with two weeks' notice. Now he's either lying in the interview or he was lying in the lobby. If I thought this person was employable, it wouldn't have been a big deal to call

Chief Pilot Jones and actually follow up, but honestly it didn't really matter what the truth was by this point.

I told him he'd been overheard explaining the circumstances of his resignation and it was pretty different from what he'd just said.

It took a few seconds for him to make all the connections, and when he did his face turned as white as a mime. The train wreck continued for the rest of the interview. He knew nothing. I suspected Chief Pilot Jones probably was none too upset when this guy left, whatever the circumstances. Not that it mattered. You can't act like an idiot in public and expect to walk away with the job.

Minding your surroundings means paying attention to everything that's going on around you during the interview process. And not *just* on the day of the interview.

Your interview starts when you walk out of your front door. If the company is flying you in for the interview, don't get into an argument with the gate agent because they're not putting you in business class. They know you're traveling as a non-revenue passenger and most likely know *why* you're traveling. Be polite and friendly to *everyone* you meet, no matter what. Flight delayed? Take it with a smile. They seated you between a screaming baby and a 400-pound man with a flatulence problem? Just deal with it. If the whole interview process is going to take 3 days, be on your best behavior for those three days, everywhere you go and in everything you do. No exceptions.

When you get to the interview location, *mind your surroundings*. Find out where you'll be going the night before, not the morning of your interview. Talk to the hotel staff about how much time you'll need to get there. If you're staying at a company hotel or one near the interview location, they're probably familiar with interviewees staying there. Just because Google maps says it's 5 miles away and will only take 15 minutes to get there doesn't mean that applies during Monday morning rush hour traffic. For every interview I've ever done, I physically go to the interview location the night before so I know where I'm going and how long it will take to get there. Then I add a little bit onto that. It's better to be early than late, so err on the side of caution in all cases.

Every person you meet during the interview process has the potential to affect the outcome of your interview. I don't know how many times applicants would come in for an interview and cop some kind of attitude with the receptionist or one of the interns. The receptionist isn't normally part of the interview process, *until* she mentions to one of the interviewers (whom she sees every day and is on a first name basis with) that someone was a real jerk when they came in. This interviewer meets with 20 applicants a week. They can hardly remember one from the next. If the receptionist says someone is a jerk, why take a chance? Don't put yourself in this position. Your interview starts from the time you leave your house, so act accordingly.

I'll tell a story about myself. It was a potential, not actual train wreck. I was interviewing in Hong Kong, and it was a multi-day extravaganza. They flew you in (after an initial interview in New York) and the process took several more days once you got there. Part of the interview process was attending a cocktail party. It wasn't "technically" part of the process, but was supposed to be a time you could meet with the interview staff in a social setting. Let's see, dress was smart casual, i.e. jacket and tie, and you're having conversations with recruitment staff over drinks. Sounds like an interview to me. Anyway, I was having the one Tsing Tao beer I was allotting myself when some lady came up to me and struck up a conversation. I didn't think much of it, and I fell into a semi-informal conversation with her. On a subconscious level I remembered this was all part of the interview, but I wasn't consciously thinking about that while I was chatting and drinking my beer.

After we'd been talking for about 10 minutes she said, "Well, I'll be doing your interview tomorrow, so I'll see you then." And she walked off.

I felt like I'd just impaled myself on something. Ice water flowed through my veins and I think my heart actually stopped beating. I hadn't been paying very close attention to what I was saying, and I immediately went over the entire conversation in my head to see if I'd said anything stupid. After thinking about it for a minute, I was confident I hadn't train wrecked myself, and my heart resumed its normal rhythm. That lady caught me completely off guard, and my hat went off to her. I was totally primed for how to act in the interview, but the social aspect of the cocktail party almost disarmed me. As it was meant to.

During my interview the following morning, many of the questions she asked started out, "Last night you mentioned..."

On a side note, there was one applicant at the cocktail party who had at least 7 Jack and Cokes by my count. I only started counting because I saw him go back for his third drink and thought that was pretty aggressive, all things considered. By number 7, he was totally hammered and all the other applicants, myself included, were doing everything we could to avoid being dragged into the ever-louder conversation he was having with anyone who would listen.

I mention this because it was the first time I ever said the following words to myself, "This is like watching a train wreck, and I can't look away. It's fascinating."

As you can imagine, I never saw him again after that night. Mind your surroundings.

Points to remember

✓ Be friendly and professional to each and every person you meet during the interview process. No exceptions.

✓ No matter what happens, do not get drawn into inappropriate actions or conversations at any point during your interview process. Do not use profanity. Do not have a conversation with someone who's speaking inappropriately; get as far away from them as possible.

Save the jokes for later

Everyone likes to be entertaining, I suppose. Over the course of your interview, you may relate an amusing story, and your interviewers may laugh (with you, hopefully, instead of at you). That's great. Relating an amusing story is not, however, the same as telling a joke in an interview. The interview joke is a rare animal, kind of like a pygmy three-toed sloth, but they're still lurking around out there. Unfortunately.

I had a client who wanted to tell a joke in the interview. He thought it would be a great way to break the ice. No matter what I said, I could not dissuade him. His gut told him it was the right thing to do, and he was going to do it, no matter what I said.

I said, "Fine, let me hear the joke."

It started out something like, "A woman walks into a bar with a salami in one hand and a stack of hundred dollar bills in the other..."

I stopped him right there and said I wasn't going to honor the money-back guarantee for the interview prep if he told that joke in the interview. That made an impression, because he said he'd think about it. I hoped he would eventually reconsider, because he had a great personality and good knowledge aside from possibly a judgment issue due to this joke fixation.

He called me after the interview to tell me how it went, and he'd decided to go with the joke. Sigh.

Right at the beginning of the interview, one of the two interviewers asked him to tell a little about himself. He asked if they'd like to hear a joke. They said sure, and he proceeded with, " A woman walks into a bar..."

When he concluded the joke with the big punch line, they sat there staring at him with completely straight faces. No one even cracked a smile.

They moved on to the next question like the joke had never happened, which was, "Why do you want to come to XYZ airlines?"

But it did happen.

The client said after the joke bombed, he felt incredibly uncomfortable and the whole thing went downhill from there.

He learned his lesson. At a subsequent interview with another company where he *didn't* do the joke thing, he was successful. Again, expensive lesson for him; missed opportunities and all that.

If that example isn't clear enough, I'll come out and say it: If you're not interviewing for a job as a stand-up comic, don't tell jokes in the interview. I've never heard of this having a positive outcome.

Practice makes perfect

You can't perform at your peak if you don't practice. Look at any athlete you watch on TV. How many hours of practice do you think it's taken for them to get to the level they're at? It's the same thing with flying an airplane; good skills don't just spontaneously appear. They have to be formed, honed, and maintained. The aspects of verbal and non-verbal communication are a skill set you need to develop, just like any other. You can't develop them if you don't practice, and just sitting around thinking about them isn't practice.

Start working this stuff into your daily life. Try to make it the normal way you interact with people, and then on interview day you won't be doing anything that isn't already natural. If you don't have to expend a lot of your thought process on keeping your presentation tight, you'll have more capacity to focus on bigger and better things.

Points to remember

✓ You need to practice your presentation and body language just like you practice your answers. Record yourself on video to get a third-person perspective for how you're coming across.

✓ Practice giving your answers in a smooth, conversational tone. Avoid saying "um" and "ah" as much as possible.

✓ Sit up straight and put both feet flat on the floor. If you have any nervous habits (rocking, swaying, fidgeting, etc.), work on avoiding them during your practice session.

✓ Fold your hands and place them either in your lap or on the interview table.

Part 4

The General Airline Interview

What in the heck are they looking for?

This is the most common question I get from people doing interview preparation: What are they looking for? It's a logical question. You're walking into a situation where you're being evaluated. You need to know how to score points if you want to win the game.

Part of the process is quantifiable. You need to meet certain minimum standards in the simulator or on the written test (if the company uses these). If your simulator performance meets the minimums, you're good. If you need an 80% on the written test and you get an 80%, you're good. All those evaluation items are black and white. You either hit the mark or you don't.

Another portion of the interview, a big portion, is not measureable by those standards. You can nail the simulator, ace the written test, and snap back answers to every technical question they ask you and still not get the job. Why not? What's the big picture?

There was a time in aviation when the majority of accidents were caused by mechanical failures and unreliable technology. You had to be able to shoot an NDB approach into mountainous terrain during a thunderstorm with monochromatic radar, because that would really happen. You had to know how to fly a partial panel approach because there were times when your instruments *would* fail. Again, that's not *could* but *would*. Pilots had to be extremely technically proficient and that was the emphasis of the old school screening. It didn't matter if the guy was a raging a-hole. He could fly the hell out of the airplane and that was all that did matter. The captain was God and you (as the potential first officer) were supposed to sit down, shut up, and not touch anything. Don't bring up the fact the airplane is running out of fuel, the captain knows what he's doing. The captain was in total control of every flight, all the way to the crash site. Then one day you got to be captain, and you could fly the hell out of the airplane (you thought), and now everybody had to listen to you. Finally. Now sit down, shut up, and don't touch anything because it's my turn. Ah, the good ole' days.

Thankfully, aircraft and technology have evolved, and so has airline philosophy for the most part. These advancements in technology have produced a separate set of problems, which have begun to manifest themselves more and more recently: an over-reliance on all this nifty automation we have. The majority of accidents recently have been attributed to breakdowns in communication and crews being too reliant on automation. These accidents are directly attributable to human factors instead of the mechanical failures of old. Translated: most accidents today happen because someone makes a mistake, not because the airplane can't fly anymore.

In most modern accidents, at least one crewmember had information that could have saved the flight, but either didn't share it or didn't communicate it effectively. If crewmembers not working together effectively cause the majority of accidents nowadays, what do you think interviewers are looking for? They are looking for people who can fly an airplane, but also people who can communicate effectively and work well with others.

Yes, they want pilots who can fly. If the captain can't leave his seat to go to the bathroom because they don't trust you at the controls, that's a problem. Yes, there is a baseline level of technical knowledge they expect you to have. They need to put you in new hire training and not have to teach you how to fly an instrument approach. What they also want to see is that you can work well with others. They need to know you'll listen to other crewmembers, as well as speak up when you see something is not right.

Interviewers realize you are human and will make mistakes. They are too. They need to know how you will manage and mitigate the mistakes you make. They need to see how you solve problems and how you prioritize multiple problems. You have to show them, by the time you leave the interview, that there is no situation you cannot deal with and no crewmember you cannot work with. You need to show your interviewers they can put their entire family on one of your flights and have no question whatsoever about their safety.

Major components to forming the right opinion in the minds of your interviewers are the concepts we've discussed up to this point. Sending the right message through your paperwork, body language, and a great attitude will get you almost half way, but not all the way. You can have a great presentation, but if you don't have the knowledge to back it up you might as well show up to the interview in your pajamas.

Once you're satisfied with your performance in the areas we've already talked about, you're ready for the meat and potatoes. It's time to hit the substance behind the appearance.

The rest of the process we'll discuss is the interview itself. You want to ace the interview? Everyone does. It's not as hard as it sounds, and here are 4 things you can start doing right now to get ready:

1. Research your upcoming interview process.
2. Focus your preparation on the areas the *company* emphasizes.
3. Start compiling experiences from your past that are good to relate in an interview.
4. Practice out loud.

Airlines are like people. They each have a different personality. Their interviews may focus on different areas, but they all want the same basic product. Some companies don't have simulator evaluations. Some companies don't have technical questions. Bullet point number 1 is research your upcoming interview. Lucky for you there is an unprecedented amount of company specific interview information out there today, maybe even *too* much. The trick is to know where to go, what's important, and how to use it. Let's start there.

Points to remember

✓ You must show your interviewers there is no situation you cannot deal with and no one you cannot work with.

Research your interview

My grandfather used to tell me stories about how hard life was when he was young, in an effort to make me appreciate how easy mine was today. He had to walk uphill to school both ways barefoot in the snow with nothing to eat but shoe leather. You know the deal. I hate to fall into that same tradition, but I want to impress on you how much easier preparing for an interview is today from just 10 years ago. There is literally more airline interview information on the Internet today than you can use.

When I was preparing for my first major airline interview, there was very little specific information out there. There were some companies around that maintained question banks on airline interviews. You went to one of these companies and paid them to get a mock interview using the questions they had compiled. The quality of the mock interview was related directly to the interest level of the person doing it, and it varied. You hoped they were giving you the right questions, you hoped they were giving you good feedback on the mock interview, and in the end you hoped it would all be enough to get the job. Lots of hoping involved in that whole process.

There were also individuals who specialized in prepping for specific companies. If you had an interview with United Airlines you went to see a certain lady, and she was supposed to have the inside track on what their process was all about. I had an interview with Northwest Airlines, and I went to a certain lady who specialized in Northwest.

You may remember I alluded to this situation in the introduction. The lady I went to was very good in some areas, and had some good insights into the specific process that you couldn't get anywhere else. She was not a pilot, however, and admitted she couldn't give me any guidance on technical questions, other than just giving me the questions.

That was fine with me. I thought just having the questions would be enough.

When I showed up for the interview, the first question they asked me was if I'd done interview prep with this particular lady. I got the immediate impression from the way they asked that this was a negative thing. But, never lie in an interview, and I answered that I had. That did not make them happy, and I know because they came out and said so. I felt like the interview was getting off on the wrong foot immediately, and I started sweating under my suit as the room seemed to be closing in around me. I figured I had two options: A) Curl up in the fetal position and start rocking back and forth, hoping they would just take pity on me, or B) Just be honest and talk to them like they were real people, which they were.

In an effort to try to salvage my opportunity, I added (honestly), "I did the prep with her because I really value this opportunity and I didn't want to leave any stone unturned in getting ready for it. If I'd known that doing interview prep with her was something you didn't approve of, I wouldn't have done it. I think she needs to start disclosing that to people before they do the prep with her."

They looked around the table at each other (there were 3 people on this particular panel interview), and kind of nodded. Then, they explained to me this lady was getting information from someplace directly in the hiring department, and they didn't appreciate it. I responded that, having working in hiring myself, I understood how important maintaining the integrity of the process was. I'm not sure what I really even meant by that, but everyone smiled and nodded and suddenly the interview was back on track.

With one notable exception: the interviewers knew where I'd done the interview prep. They obviously knew what questions the prep lady had gone over beforehand because they did not ask me one single question I'd been given by her.

116

If listening to this lady's interview prep were all I'd done to prepare, I would be summarizing another interview train wreck right here. In addition to the prep, however, I used my own system and did my own research. That system involved finding out what subject areas Northwest Airlines thought were important in the interview process, and preparing for those subjects, not just for specific questions.

At the time that was more difficult than it sounds, and took a lot of networking and legwork. Ultimately everything worked out in the end, so all the time and effort was well spent.

The good news for you, today, is that researching the interview process for a particular company has never been easier. There are some fantastic websites out there with all the information you need to take control of your own future and make sure you're successful. There is, in fact, so much information out there that you need to understand what's important and what's not.

Interview gouge -or just "gouge"- is slang for inside, unofficial information that gets passed on from person to person. Someone goes through an interview, writes down everything they get asked, and passes it onto the next person. All interviewers, over time, will settle into a series of subjects they like and are comfortable with. It's human nature. The actual questions themselves may change, but for the most part the core subject areas don't. If you can look back far enough at any company's interviewing history, you can get a pretty good prediction for the types of questions that will be coming your way. The top 3 interview gouge sites on the Internet right now are:

1. www.aviationinterviews.com
2. www.mypilotcareer.com
3. www.willflyforfood.cc

There are also some very active forums out there frequented by pilots currently working at the companies you are targeting. Pilots love to talk about pilot stuff, and you can usually get pretty good answers to questions you post, or get a good feel for what's going on just by reading active discussion. Keep in mind; this information you are getting from the Internet is posted anonymously, so take everything you read with a grain of salt. The most useful forums are:

1. www.airlinepilotcentral.com
2. www.pprune.com
3. www.flightinfo.com

Forums are forums and you're probably familiar with how they work. If not, the first time you look at them they're self-explanatory. It's a bulletin board where people ask questions, make comments, and try to elicit reactions. If you find yourself stumped on something or you have a specific question, you can usually get an answer through the forums. Just make sure you perform due diligence and verify any information you get. Forums are anonymous, and you can't be sure of the quality of information you're getting.

It's best to start doing a little bit of research on the companies you're applying to before you actually get the interview scheduled. Read through the gouge to see what they've been asking and watch the forums for important news. If Delta Airlines suddenly schedules you for an interview in two weeks, and you haven't started getting ready *at all*, you're going to be running around with your hair on fire. It's do-able; it's just a lot of work. If you've already been looking into what's involved in the Delta interview beforehand, you'll be that much farther ahead of the game. Instead of playing catch-up, you'll be filling in the blanks to complete your preparation. Use the gouge sites to get a working knowledge of the company's interview process, and try to clear up any ambiguities by posting questions on the message boards.

One thing to be aware of: even though they may come across like ogres, the people doing interviews don't live in caves. They know these sites are out there. I used to enjoy going to them and reading what people posted after I interviewed them. A fellow interviewer and myself used to trade beers every time one of our names got posted online. Of course, posts with his name usually said "raging a-hole" after it. Well, more often anyway. What this means to you is that interviewers will change their questions, but subjects remain the same. They know the gouge is out there. They're going to try to catch you with something you're not expecting to see how you handle it. Interviewers have nothing better to do all day than sit around and come up with some question no one will be able to answer, so it will happen. Just accept it. We'll talk about how to effectively deal with that a little later.

Be careful reading user-submitted narratives. You have no idea who the user is that is posting. They say they're a competent airline pilot, and a good interviewer, but in reality they're a 600-pound shut-in with an animal porn fetish. Or the poster could just be a total idiot. They could answer every single question wrong, but they're not going to post that. They're going to post that they knew everything and had great answers, but they didn't get the job because the interviewer was a jerk. If they write a long narrative about their experience, a lot of their opinion is going to find its way into the post. You'll want to ignore the opinion, and focus on the facts you can glean from their writing.

A further caution about online gouge: Do not ever, ever, ever use an answer you got off a gouge site or forum. Here's a great example of why *not* to do this: As I said, I used to read through the gouges when I was doing interviews. Someone (not someone I had interviewed) posted his/her interview experience online, along with the answers they'd given to each question. It just so happened that most of the answers they'd

119

given were totally wrong. I noticed over the course of the next week that a higher-than-normal number of applicants were giving wrong answers to the technical questions I asked, and they were the same exact wrong answers that were posted on this gouge. Be very careful about following the herd mentality when you're reading through gouge, because the herd isn't always correct.

Interview gouge is a great tool, but like any tool it only works if you use it correctly. Do not use answers from someone else's gouge. Use interview gouge to learn where to focus your preparation efforts, not just study questions and answers. Don't let some board poster's opinion of how to answer a question influence the best answer. The best answer for you may be different from the best answer for someone else.

Points to remember

✓ Consult all the gouge you can and make sure you know exactly what events will take place during the interview. Make sure to prepare equally for each event: simulator evaluation, written tests, and the interview itself.
✓ Do not use answers you get from gouge. You *must* come up with your own answers.

Beware the short-notice interview

It is possible to get this call: "We've just had a cancellation, would you like to come in for an interview the day after tomorrow?"

There are times when companies, because of extenuating circumstances, will want to schedule your interview on short notice. Be very, very careful about accepting a short-notice interview. I won't say not to take it, every situation is different, but don't take it *unless* you're ready for it. I can guarantee you there are *not* two different interviews, the normal one and the short-notice one. You will get the same interview everyone else gets. If you've been semi-expecting a call and you're totally prepared, then go for it. If you are not ready, tell them you're not available that day and you'll need something later. Showing up without any of your documentation and blowing answers in the interview because they just called you yesterday will *absolutely not* get you any sympathy or special consideration. It will get you a thanks but no thanks letter with a return trip to the job market.

Points to remember

✓ Don't accept a short-notice interview unless you are fully and truly ready for it. You will *not* get any special consideration for showing up on short notice.

Fly the simulator like you own it

You don't have to qualify for the Apollo program, but you have to demonstrate enough proficiency in the simulator to show you're trainable.

Interview Train Wreck #12

The simulator evaluation we gave was conducted in a full-motion Canadair Regional Jet Level D Simulator. The profile consisted of a takeoff, acceleration to 250kts, steep turns, descent to holding, vectors to the ILS. There weren't any tricks involved; it was a very straightforward profile.

Two applicants at a time were evaluated. They would each take turns acting as pilot flying and pilot monitoring. The applicants for this particular session I was observing had similar backgrounds; they were flying light piston twin-engine aircraft. Neither had any glass cockpit experience. An instructor pilot was conducting the evaluation, and I was sitting in the back of the sim doodling on a clipboard.

The first applicant sat in the left seat while his partner was in the right, and we did the takeoff. That went OK. Then we leveled at 5000' and started to accelerate to 250kts. The flying pilot was trying to keep the airplane level as we accelerated, and when I say, "trying," I mean pitching up and down wildly as the altitude fluctuated +/- 1000'. Just when I thought I'd better start looking for an airsick bag (I guess in this case it would have technically been a simsick bag) he got the oscillations down to about +/- 500', which was easier for my stomach to handle. We did a steep turn to the left, and almost went inverted. The instructor took pity on him and skipped the holding, giving him a heading to intercept the ILS. We blew through the glide slope. He dove down to try to catch it, and the instructor ended the evaluation by hitting the flight freeze button just before we crashed with 45 degrees of bank and 20 degrees pitch down towards the dirt.

That, in case you're wondering, is what a bad simulator evaluation looks like.

The guy knew he'd blown it, obviously. While I felt bad for him, I didn't exactly want to fly with him, either. As the applicants were switching seats, he explained he wasn't used to the glass instrument display and was having a hard time interpreting it.

I knew the guy getting ready to fly next had the same background, and I almost excused myself from the simulator. I didn't really want to witness another bloody massacre, but there wasn't time to bring the simulator down off motion, so I was committed.

We took off, and the second guy flew the sim like it was on rails. It was the complete polar opposite of the first applicant. These two pilots had almost the exact same background, and yet there was a night and day performance difference.

Later, I asked the second guy what he'd done to prepare for the sim.

He said he and a buddy had pooled their money and rented a full-motion glass cockpit simulator for a few hours to practice. They each had enough time to get through the profile twice.

So what was the real difference between the two applicants? Preparation. He knew from the gouge what the profile would be and in what aircraft it would be. Practice. He spent the time, effort, and money to practice before he had to perform. Preparation and practice. That's it.

Back in the day, almost every company at the top of the job pyramid had a sim eval, and some of the profiles bordered on truly ridiculous (NDB holding with an engine shut down? Really?) Not all companies require a simulator evaluation nowadays, and you'll know what's coming based on researching your specific interview. Simulator events shouldn't be a big deal, because all you're really doing is exercising your core skill set. Nobody *enjoys* trying to fly an unfamiliar simulator with someone looking over your shoulder, however, the whole time deciding whether or not to hire you based on your performance. But, being a pilot is a performance-based job, there's no two ways about it. Thus an interview sim event always generates some stress. If you fly the sim like a monkey trying to copulate with a football, none of the interview strategies I've gone over here are going to matter. That's the bad news. The good news: you can fly the sim. If you have enough flight experience to apply for an airline job, you can definitely do it. Aviation is inherently unforgiving. If you were not capable of flying an airplane at all you wouldn't be sitting here reading this. You'd be the subject of an NTSB report.

Let's look at this from the interviewer's perspective: What are they looking for? Do they want you to fly an ILS approach *perfectly*, or a steep turn with zero altitude and airspeed deviation? No. They are not looking for perfection. Interviewers are looking for the overall trend in your sim evaluation to see if you are trainable to their standards. You, as the applicant, must demonstrate the minimum acceptable level of proficiency in the simulator.

Some sim evals are more subjective than others. Some are point based like a video game. Others are opinion based like an interview. Good online research through the forums and the gouge will tell you what kind you're doing. The question your interviewers are trying to answer is whether this person will be successful in our training program and meet our standards.

Nothing ticks off a company more than putting someone all the way through training, only to have them unable to pass their release-to-line check ride. Pilot applicants are investments. It's expensive and time consuming to hire and train pilots. The company ultimately wants to see a return on their investment. A pilot that isn't successful in training will never provide a return. Interviewers who consistently recommend applicants who fail training get a lot of angry phone calls from management types. If their track record is bad enough, they usually end up not being interviewers very much longer. Hence, they have a vested interest in your success. Proficiency in the simulator is the way to show them you can and will be successful.

The simulator evaluation generates a lot of anxiety for applicants. No one likes being watched and no one likes being evaluated. Lucky for you, the sim evaluation will not create any anxiety, because you are going to be totally prepared for it. Preparation reduces anxiety, which in turn improves your performance. You know how to research your interview. This includes what to expect in the sim. Since you know what's coming, the only question is how best to apply that knowledge.

There is no excuse for going into a simulator evaluation cold. Even if you are high time and high experience, you want to get up to speed on the aircraft and procedures you'll be flying. You need to walk in there totally confident in your capabilities.

The pilots with the most problems in simulator evaluations say, "I really hope this goes OK," as they cross their fingers and rub their rabbit's foot.

You need to walk into the sim with the attitude that it is only a formality to get you to the interview, and *know* you have the capability to perform, not hope.

As with all aspects of interview preparation, the most effective tools at your disposal are practice and repetition. Once you've got an idea of the profile, see which event makes you groan at the thought of it. That is the one you want to place the most emphasis on. You should also know what kind of cockpit you're going to be in. Practicing approaches in a round-dial cockpit when your evaluation will be in a glass cockpit is better than nothing, but it's not as good as practicing approaches in a glass cockpit. I can tell you from experience that the first time you see a glass cockpit, if you're not accustomed to one, it's confusing. The setup is totally different from what you're used to, and there is a steep learning curve. Once you become accustomed to them, glass cockpits provide infinitely more and better information. Don't just assume that since you're an ace on old style gauges, and everyone says glass cockpits are better, you'll be an ace on a glass cockpit without ever having flown one. The first time I transitioned to a glass cockpit I had no idea what I was supposed to be looking at. I had a tendency to fixate on one particular item, but I had no idea what it was telling me.

The inverse is also true. While becoming ever more rare, there's a chance you can go in the opposite direction. If you've been flying a glass cockpit for a while and you're going to be evaluated in an old-school cockpit, you may want to brush up on your round dial procedures. This has happened to me twice. I was flying a glass cockpit CRJ and had an interview where I had to fly a Boeing 747 Classic simulator. Again when I was flying the 747-400, I had to do an interview sim evaluation in the 747 Classic. Going back to round gauges when you're used to glass can affect your performance.

Even switching from one glass display to another can be disorientating. I'd been flying the 747-400 for years, and had an interview sim evaluation in the MD-11. The MD-11 was just different enough that if I hadn't practiced on it, I don't think it would have gone as well as I would have liked. And there's the rub. How do you practice flying a sim for your interview? Or more importantly, how do you do it in a cost effective manner?

There are generally two options for sim preparation, depending on your interview profile. Some companies use full-motion simulators, others use a computer based simulator. Those are the same options you have available for practice. You can prepare for your interview simulator evaluation by:

1. Renting a full motion simulator. Renting a simulator is expensive, but it's the real deal.
2. Flying a computer based simulator. This option is cheaper and you can do it over and over. It is not, however, the total experience of a full motion simulator.

the full motion simulator

Obviously, if you'll be flying a computer-based sim for your interview, you're not interested in full-motion simulators. If you're going to be flying a full motion sim, however, renting one is a great way to prepare. You'll never get a better dry run for your interview than actually doing it in the full-motion sim. The downsides are it's incredibly expensive, and you don't get much time for your money. You'll only get a couple of hours for several hundred dollars, but it's a very valuable couple of hours. You can run through the complete interview profile maybe 3 times in 2 hours, depending on the profile. More importantly, it will give you a huge confidence boost going into the interview. If you have zero sim experience and the sim evaluation is causing you a lot of anxiety, I would recommend this.

Remember, if you're going to bite the bullet and spend the money for a full-motion sim experience, you are the customer. You are in charge of what happens in the sim on your nickel. The company you're renting the sim from may have the interview profile for the particular company, or they may not. I know people that have paid a lot of money for a sim and shown up expecting the instructor to know what they needed to do. The instructor had no idea and they just did a generic profile. The instructors will do their best, but they can't cover everything you need for your interview if they have no idea what the profile is going to be. Create your own profile that efficiently covers all the maneuvers you'll be doing for your interview. When you show up for your sim block, hand it to the instructor and tell them you want to get through this profile as many times as possible. If you run through the profile once or twice and feel good about it, finish up repeating whatever areas you feel are your weakest.

The more people you have and the more time you purchase, the less expensive the sim time. If you decide renting a full-motion sim is what you need to do to prepare, find other applicants in the same boat using the forums listed earlier. Get a group together and it will be cheaper for everyone.

The computer based simulator

When I was getting ready for my Cathay Pacific interview, I got in touch with a network of other pilots in the same situation through message boards. The interview was to be conducted in the Boeing 747 Classic full-motion sim in Hong Kong. A number of these pilots were getting together and renting a full-motion 747 Classic sim in Miami, to the tune of around $500 for a couple of hours. Unfortunately for me, I've been conditioned by years of free USA Today newspapers and airline crew breakfast buffets. I can't spend $500 on anything that doesn't involve more speed than common sense. When all those guys headed to Miami, I decided I had to come up with an alternative.

I'm going to qualify this and say I'm not a huge computer gamer. My computer didn't have any kind of super-trick liquid-cooled video card processor or anything like that. I didn't have the aircraft yoke/throttle

128

combo set-up. I simply went out and bought a copy of Microsoft Flight Simulator at Best Buy, and a USB joystick. Next, I searched around online and found a 747 Classic downloadable add-on that cost around $30. It had pretty simple installation instructions, which I followed to the letter, and the next thing I knew I had a computer-based 747 Classic simulator with 24-hour access. All for around $100. I incorporated flying the computer sim into my study sessions, going through the interview profile once in the morning, and then once at night. After a few days, I started getting bored with the whole profile and I cut it back to once at night. Then I got bored with that and I just started shooting an approach and doing some holding pattern entries.

When I got to Hong Kong and sat in that 747 Classic simulator, I was totally comfortable. It was just like sitting in front of my computer back home, the only differences were the joystick was now a yoke and I had four throttles to move around. I actually started getting bored during the interview sim. My mind began wandering to where I was going for dinner that night, how I would answer this interview question or that interview question, until the little voice in my head that keeps me out of trouble yelled, "Hey smart guy, stay focused!"

All in all, it was the strongest interview sim I've ever flown. I attribute it directly to the practice I had on the computer.

The first time I walk into the cockpit of a jet I've never flown before, I'm reminded of a line from the fantastic movie *Fear and Loathing in Las Vegas*, "The dashboard was filled with esoteric lights and gauges that I would never understand."

This pretty much sums up my feelings in an unfamiliar cockpit. Everything looks wrong, I feel clumsy and slow as I fumble around unfamiliar territory, and I have a tendency to fixate. This isn't the situation you want to find yourself in on interview day. If you become accustomed to the cockpit and instrument layout by looking at it over and over on a computer screen, that's the next best thing to flying it. Setting up your own computer-based sim will increase your comfort level and proficiency by leaps and bounds. Even if you go out and rent a full-motion sim, I still recommend practicing on a computer because it absolutely *will* improve your performance on interview day.

The simulator portion of an interview is a major component as to whether you get hired or not. You won't get hired unless you provide the minimum acceptable level of performance. However, no matter how well you interview, you don't want to aim for the minimum. You want your interviewer to walk out of the sim with absolutely no doubt in their mind about how you can fly. Don't leave anything to chance. Make sure you are comfortable and confident in how you'll perform when you sit down in the sim. The only way to ensure your performance is to practice, practice, practice.

Points to remember

✓ After researching your interview, put together a maneuver profile to practice. Know in what type of sim - full-motion or computer based- the evaluation will be conducted.

✓ Practice the maneuver profile *in the aircraft you'll be flying*. Find a full-motion sim (spendy) or download a simulator for your computer (not-so-spendy). Practice, practice, practice. When you're so sick of the profile you don't think you can get through it again without smashing your head through the monitor, do it one more time.

✓ Did I mention practice?

Part 5

The technical interview

Impressing your interviewers with technical knowledge is an easy way to demonstrate competence and proficiency. Give clear, concise, and correct answers to technical questions and you'll make a great overall impression.

Interview Train Wreck #13

I sat down with the interviewee, a very personable gentleman who was currently flying single pilot charter operations in the northeastern U.S. He was visibly nervous, so I thought we'd go over some basic technical questions, just to help him get into the groove.

I pulled out an ILS approach chart and asked him to brief it like he was setting up to shoot it. The best way to brief a chart is basically to start at the top and hit all the pertinent information on the way down. If you're operating in a multi crew environment, this becomes second nature. This interviewee was coming from a single-pilot environment, however. His brief was very disjointed, choppy, and he left out a lot of the important stuff. He briefed every radio frequency and navigation aid on the chart, but forgot the big-ticket items like what the decision height was or what visibility he needed for the approach. I chocked this up to the fact he didn't normally do approach briefings.

I asked him where he would start the missed approach procedure. Going missed on an ILS is about as basic as it gets. I really only asked so I could think of another question while he answered. I was lost in thought about what my next question would be when it dawned on me that he still hadn't answered.

He was studying the chart intently.

"When you get the time...right down here...uh...2 minutes and 31 seconds."

"That's for the localizer only approach," I said. "If you're doing the full ILS, where is the missed approach point?"

After another long pause he let out a sigh like he'd been holding his breath, "I don't know. I thought it was from the time."

Now all the red flags went up. I'm immediately picturing myself in the back of this guy's airplane as he's shooting an approach down to minimums, with no idea what to do if he gets there and doesn't see the runway. We level off at 200 feet and mow the grass while he's waiting for 2 minutes and 31 seconds to tick by...I guess. Would that really happen? Who knows? But that's the impression his answer gave, and that's all that counts.

But, like I said before, the guy was personable and I liked him (remember, interviewers work for you or against you). I gave him the benefit of the doubt and hoped he was just having an attack of nerves.

"OK, let's forget about this approach for a second," I said, pulling the plate off the table. "How much fuel do you need on the airplane for a flight?"

Long pause.

"I've never done airline operations before, I'm not sure what you're asking," he said.

Now the flags that went up a little earlier have been replaced by a loud warning horn sounding in my head.

"Don't worry about airline stuff. You're operating single pilot part 135 charter, right?"

"Yes."

Well, at least he knew that.

"When you load the people up in your airplane, how much fuel do you need onboard before you depart? Don't worry about airline rules. What do YOU need for YOUR part 135 flight? Legally."

"I usually put on about 50 gallons."

"And how far can you fly on that?" I ask.

Keep in mind I have only a vague understanding of FAR part 135, having no firsthand experience with it. However, I'm pretty sure I know what the fuel requirements are for an IFR flight. Something like fly to destination, fly to your alternate, then 45 minutes thereafter.

"Oh...I can get to airport XYZ and back with that much." Long pause.

I think my facial tick must have started up, because at this point he realized he was in way over his head.

"You know, anything I don't know right now, I can learn. I have to get out of this place I'm at. It's terrible. I really need this job," he pleaded.

But what did he really expect me to do for him in this situation?

Had he done anything to <u>try</u> to get this job? He didn't really know how to operate his own airplane, is he really going to take the time to learn how to operate a more complex one? Is something going to change in his motivation between his previous job and this one? As the magic 8-ball would say, "signs point to no."

I can hear the phone call from the training department already: "Why did you recommend this guy, exactly? We're burning all our sim time learning basic IFR procedures. Your interviewing...sucks."

You can beg and plead and try to rely on the sympathy of your interviewers only so much. They can like you. They can even pull for you to a certain degree. At the end of your interview, however, if they have the slightest reservation about your skills or knowledge, you've missed the mark.

Airline training is often (accurately) described as trying to take a drink from a fire hose. There is no time to go back and learn the basics. Too much information is coming at you like an avalanche accelerating downhill. There was no doubt in my mind this gentleman wouldn't be successful in training, and that would put him in an even worse situation.

In an effort to help him out, I told him flat out that I couldn't recommend him, and why. I told him that if he worked on certain areas he could come back and re-interview in 6 months and probably be successful.

This was the first time (but not the last) I saw a grown man cry at the interview table.

Interview Train Wreck #14

I was interviewing an applicant and we got onto the subject of runway lighting.

"Where do the runway edge lights turn amber?" I asked.

"The last 3000 feet of the runway," he responded.

"Actually, something happens to the centerline lights at 3000 feet. Do you know what that is?" He'd been doing OK on the technical stuff, and I was actually trying to give him a hint. Apparently he didn't take it that way.

"No. The edge lights change at 3000 feet, the centerline lights go red and white at 2000 feet. You're mixing them up," he said with total conviction.

I was pretty sure I wasn't, since I'd asked that question about 150 times. The interview rooms doubled as classrooms, and there happened to be a copy of the Aeronautical Information Manual sitting in the corner. The dynamic of the interview had shifted.

"We can look it up in the AIM, if you think I'm wrong," I said.

I motioned toward the book. When someone missed a question I normally just moved on, but I was curious how this was going to play out.

"Yeah, I don't think you're right," he said, grabbing the book.

Fair enough. It was possible I'd gotten it mixed up since the last interview 30 minutes ago. I sat back and studied my fingernails while he flipped through the tome. After a minute, I heard the book snap shut and it thumped back onto the table.

"You were right. The edge lights change at 2000 feet."

"I thought maybe I was. Thanks for checking," I said.

I'm all for sticking to your guns when the chips are down, but you had better be sure you're right. Absolutely sure.

Getting into an argument, or even a disagreement, with your interviewer is kind of like getting into an argument with your check airman, or the cop pulling you over for speeding. You're never going to win, because they're the ones filling out the paperwork. They will always have the last word. The best-case scenario is that you're right, but you come off as argumentative and kind of a jerk. The worst-case scenario is you make your interviewer feel stupid and you come off as kind of a jerk. Jerk is not a good impression choice to leave them with.

There are two main types of questions you will get in your interview: technical or HR/situational. Right now we're going to focus on the technical.

So what is a technical question really? A technical question is anything with a quantifiable right or wrong answer. It can be related to aviation, or it can come completely out of left field.

"What's the definition of angle of attack?"

That has a right or wrong answer, you either know it or you don't. Technical question.

"How do you compute the area of a circle?"

You either know pi R squared or you don't. Technical.

"Tell me about one of your faults."

There's no right answer to that, just right or wrong *ways* to answer. That's a human resource question.

A lot of people dread technical interviews. You should love them. You need to get excited about technical questions. Given the choice, I'll take a technical interview every time. There is no subjectivity to technical questions. It's obvious to everyone in the room whether you know the answers or not. Sitting in the interview chair, snapping correct answers back as quickly as they can ask them makes you look like a rock star. Oh baby, I'm getting excited just thinking about it. Weird...I know.

As you may remember from earlier, you're not reading *The Quick and Easy Guide to Scam Your Interviewers and Fool Them Into Hiring You.* Maybe you meant to get that book and wound up with this one by mistake. That works out better for you. *How to Land a Top Paying Airline Job* works all the time, and teaches you how to ensure your success. *The Quick and Easy Guide* only works part of the time. Preparing for an interview the *right* way requires some time and effort. But, when compared with the time and effort it's taken you to get to this point in your career, it's not really that much.

There are books out there that claim to tell you how to "ace technical interviews" and contain all the information you'll ever need. The reality is there isn't *one single* book out there that will answer all your questions. There are books and study guides that can give you a good foundation to build on, but a generic study guide can only take you so far. Study guides have value, but don't make the mistake of putting all your eggs in that one basket. If you don't narrow the focus of what you really need to know, you're shooting in the dark and hoping what you study is what they'll ask. We don't want to deal in hopes. We want to deal in absolutes.

What to study

The dread of the technical interview stems from mankind's inherent fear of the unknown. What are they going to ask? Am I studying the right thing? What if they ask me something I have no idea how to answer? You don't want to miss the job opportunity, but you want to avoid looking like a dumbass even more. Here's the good news: there are only two places you need to go to figure out what you have to study:

1. Your current operation
2. The interview gouge

Your current operation and past experiences are your greatest assets. Why? No matter what type of operation you're currently conducting, you deal with the following technical areas on a daily basis:

✓ Regulations
✓ Instrument procedures
✓ Weather
✓ Performance
✓ Aircraft systems

Now guess what? These particular areas form the bulk of most technical interviews. You can (and should) incorporate studying for your interview into your daily operations, starting today. The next time you're looking at an approach plate, go through it carefully from top to bottom. Do you understand what every symbol means?

Hey, what's that little circle R next to the approach frequency? I've never actually noticed that before. At your next opportunity, follow up on your knowledge gaps and fill them in. Over time, you'll find the gaps getting smaller and smaller.

The introduction section of Jeppesen Charts contains a wealth of information. You should go through it *at least* a couple of times if you're getting ready to interview. Can you *confidently* get yourself from the IFR airway system to the initial approach, shoot the approach, and continue to the holding pattern following the missed approach procedure? If not, go back to the introduction section.

You're reviewing the weather before a flight; can you decode and interpret every single item in a surface observation and forecast? Don't cheat yourself. I know there's a couple of sections of obscure text on there you glance over because you don't fully understand it (because I've glanced over it, too).

Working performance numbers for your flight; do you *fully* understand what every performance number means and what guarantees those numbers give you? If you do understand it, can you effectively explain it? If not, look it up.

If you do this diligently for a few weeks leading up to your interview, you'll be amazed at how far you expand your knowledge base. Once you move on to step two (reviewing the gouge) you'll be surprised at how basic a lot of it seems.

Using this method of preparing helps in a couple of ways. First, you will, without a doubt, get questions about what you're currently doing. Second, you *have* to be able to talk intelligently and confidently about your current operations.

Example:

I was interviewing an applicant who was currently flying the ATR. I had been a captain on the ATR, previously. I couldn't remember that much about it (I have truly remarkable capabilities for dumping information! It's almost a superpower...), aside from a few limitations and the fact that it had an AC Wild power system. I asked the applicant what the maximum takeoff weight was. He got within several thousand pounds, but was very vague and evasive for someone currently operating the aircraft. The max takeoff weight is kind of an important number that's nice to know. I asked him how the AC Wild power system worked. Again, not a very clear understanding of the system. If he didn't know much about his current aircraft, was he really going to put much effort into learning a new one if we hired him? Probably not.

I've seen this numerous times. An applicant who's flying a Lear jet comes in. One of the guys on the panel has time in Lear jets and asks a question about a system or limitation. The applicant sits there like we just asked him to give a brief rundown on The Theory of Relativity. You <u>have</u> to know your current operation and aircraft, because someone doing your interview might know it, too.

In addition to being ready for questions about your current operation, there is another advantage to knowing this stuff cold: you will fall back on your current operational knowledge in times of crisis. Times of crisis are when you have no earthly idea what the heck your interviewers are talking about. This is an incredibly useful tool, and I can't overstate how important it is to fall back on this.

When a question comes up you don't know the answer to, instead of giving your interviewers the deer in headlights look, mentally put yourself in the seat you're currently operating. Give an intelligent answer about how you would approach this problem from your current operational perspective. You can't throw your hands up and admit defeat in real life; you always need to come up with a solution. Use the tools you have available, like you would on any normal operational day.

Here's a personal example of what I'm talking about:

I was interviewing in New York with a world-class international carrier. I would argue with anyone that this was (and is still) one of the most technically demanding interviews in the world today. One subject they were known to ask about (from the gouge) was the fuel system on the 747-400. At this point in my career, I had zero experience on that particular airframe. In the years immediately following September 11th 2001, it was very difficult to get aircraft systems information. It's still difficult to find anything official. I found some unofficial gouge about the fuel system on some forums, but nothing solid enough that I was willing to bet my interview on. I kind of blew this subject area off and just hoped they wouldn't ask about it.

Murphy's Law is always in effect at all times in interview situations. If you purposely don't study something (and I still don't know how they know), that is the line of questioning you'll get. It wasn't the first question I got, but it was close.

"How does the fuel system on the 747-400 work?"

My mental response was: Oh...great.

Time to initiate Plan B.

I said, "I don't have any experience with the 747-400, but this is how it works on the CRJ..."

I hadn't heard of anyone trying this before in this particular interview, but I figured it was better than just saying I didn't know.

So, I gave them a nauseatingly detailed description of how the CRJ fuel system worked. The check airman on the pilot side of the interview seemed pretty pleased with that. I ultimately got invited to Hong Kong for phase II of the interview process.

Always fall back on your current operational experience and knowledge. These experiences you've built up to this point in your career are some of your greatest assets. Even if you feel like you don't have that many, I'll bet it's much more applicable than you think. Use them.

The interview gouge

Interview gouge comes in all shapes and sizes. It can be as simple as talking to a friend of a friend who interviewed recently, or as complex as combing through the internet compiling every question you can find that has ever been asked by your prospective company.

Keep in mind, recruiting departments HATE the fact that easy access to interview gouge exists. They do everything in their power to limit the information that gets leaked. It's not uncommon lately to require applicants to sign non-disclosure agreements concerning the interview process, but it seems like the information leaks out slowly over time, regardless. So, how do you separate what's important from what's not? That is the two million dollar question (two million dollars again...why does he keep using that number? That's roughly the industry-average career earnings difference between top paying companies and those that aren't).

I could easily quadruple the size of this book by including every technical question you could possibly be asked. And there are books out there that attempt to do that.

To me that's like saying, "Hey, you want to study for a spelling bee? Just study this Webster's dictionary. Everything you need to know is in here."

That's not very realistic. It's also why generalized study guides can only help so much. You need to separate the wheat from the chaff, and figure out areas the company focuses on, because then you can focus on those areas, specifically.

Airlines are like people. They each have a different personality. One airline places a lot of emphasis on instrument approach charts and procedures. Another company won't even pull out a chart. One airline gives you a written test with geometry problems. Another company doesn't even give a test. You need to know what the particular airline you're interviewing with wants to see, and that is where the gouge is valuable. There are websites out there that literally list every question asked at a particular company for over a decade. Just type "airline interview gouge" into Google and you'll see the big 3 immediately. Even if the gouge isn't that current, take the time to go back and look at the *trend* in subject areas, and the things that are important to this particular company will become obvious.

When I was preparing for an interview in Hong Kong, one subject I kept reading different variations of in the gouge was: "What type of engines do our (insert aircraft type here) have?"

This is nothing I would ever have looked into, normally. I kept seeing it pop up on the gouge, however, going back several years. I've never been asked an interview question like this at any other airline I've interviewed for. Frankly, it didn't seem the least bit important to me. CF6, JT8, RB211...they're all just a jumble of numbers and letters to me. I push throttle, airplane go fast. Knowing the engine types is important to this particular company, however. That means if you have an interview there, the engine types are important to you.

So, I learned about the engines they used at this company; all the engines, not just the ones I'd seen asked about in the gouge, which was a good thing, because the question I got was a general, "Tell us everything you know about our different fleet types."

Since I had studied a subject area, instead of an individual question, I knew all about the engines they used. I didn't know *exactly* what the question would be when I was studying, only that it would have something to do with which engines they used.

This is where I see people make the biggest mistake with the gouge. They print out all the interview gouge they can get their hands on, and then find answers to the questions they see there. But *only* those questions. Then they study those questions and answers over and over again and think they're prepared. But, (and this is the point you want to take away from this section) *you will not get the exact questions you see on the gouge*. You may get a couple, but no more than that. Like I said before, interviewers don't live in caves, and they know gouge is out there no matter how hard they try to control it. They're not going to ask the *exact* same questions over and over again. They will typically ask different variations of questions you've read on the gouge. This is where you can use gouge effectively and where others won't: the questions almost always revolve around the same *subject matter*. Use the gouge to narrow down the *subject matter* you study, not the questions.

Get on the gouge sites, search forums, and find out what areas the company focuses on. Those are the areas you need to focus on. Understand where you need to fill in the blanks of the knowledge base you've been building and you'll be able to cope with any situation they throw at you.

Study subject matter, not questions

You don't learn effectively by sitting down and memorizing questions and answers. That works fine for basic concepts with one or two word answers, but the more complex the questions get, the less effective that method is. I've never taken this approach to preparing for an interview, and I've never taught it to anyone I prepped. That's why well over 95% of the people I prep are successful. Studying questions and answers works fine if they're the exact questions and answers you're going to get. In an interview setting, you can never count on that.

If you've ever taken an FAA written test, which if you're reading this I'm guessing you have, there's a good chance you've read the work of Irvin N. Gleim. Irvin is a great author and nearly everyone who takes these tests reads his work. Why? Is it because of his entertaining stories and snappy prose? Not likely. Everyone reads these books because Gleim reproduces every question that could possibly be on your written test, *verbatim*. You spend a few days reading the questions and answers over and over again, and when you show up for the test, you don't even have to read the entire question before you know the answer. You get a 97% and walk out the door patting yourself on the back about what an accomplished pilot you've become.

A few days after your written test, if someone asked you the formula for shifting loaded palettes on a 727 (actually, I don't know if that's still on there, but it was when I took it), you'd laugh out loud. You only stored all those questions in your short-term memory, passed the test, and then dumped it.

Imagine you took a slightly different test, and you used Gleim's guide to study for it. Pretend they kept the same *content*, but re-worded all the questions. Not a lot, but just enough that you had to apply knowledge rather than regurgitating what you'd crammed into your head. Would you still get that 97%? I know I probably wouldn't.

Being effective in an interview means you need to be able to apply knowledge, not just regurgitate facts.

Here's the beak down on how to effectively prepare for an interview once you get the call, or if you're expecting the call, or if you just want to start getting ready now and not be under the gun when the time comes. It will set you apart from the other applicants who just memorize answers:

1. Go online and start compiling the gouge for that company.

2. Spool up your professional network and find out if anyone knows anyone who's interviewed recently.

3. Separate all the questions you can get your hands on into technical and non-technical ones.

4. Break the technical questions down into *subject areas*. List each question in an applicable area, i.e. performance, weather, FARs, miscellaneous, etc. This will be your interview study sheet.

5. Once you have everything organized, go through the questions. If you read a question and you're not *completely* sure of the answer, circle it. By completely sure, I mean you have the ability to explain it to someone who doesn't understand it. Once you've been through the gouge and you have a bunch of circled questions, go and find the answers to these questions yourself. There is no substitute for actually pouring through the books on your own to get this information. Once you find an answer to one of your questions, make sure you understand *why* it is the correct answer. Write down the entire concept behind this question on your study sheet.

6. As you look for a particular answer, you'll come across related information you're not familiar with. When you read something you don't fully understand, *don't just glance over it.* Follow up until you do understand it. The act of researching one answer this way increases your knowledge base exponentially. The more you do it, the less time it will take to find subsequent answers.

When I'm preparing for the technical portion of an interview, I reference these four publications more than any others:

1. <u>Federal Aviation Regulations</u> (or applicable for your operations)
2. <u>Aeronautical Information Manual</u>
3. The introduction section to Jeppesen Charts. There is a wealth of information on chart symbology, instrument procedures, communications, and more.
4. Aerodynamics for Naval Aviators. I first had to read this for a college course, and I absolutely hated it. It's very, very dry. However, the aerodynamics and performance information you can get out of this book is very valuable and worth the effort.

Here's an example of how this system worked for me in real life:

I was never a big performance guy. Company X asked a lot of performance questions, and I saw V1 mentioned in the gouge a lot. I thought I had a pretty good idea of what V1 meant, but I wanted to actually *see* the exact definition. In doing so, I came across the term Vmu.

"What the heck is Vmu?"

So I looked up Vmu. Vmu is minimum un-stick speed, the speed at which an aircraft can safely lift off the runway and continue takeoff...blah blah...OK got it. I made a little note about it on my study guide and on I went. Flash forward to the interview. I can still see the whole process unfold.

I'm assuming my interviewer probably had asked, "What's the definition of V1" so many times that if he did it once more, his head would have actually, physically, exploded.

So, he decided to change it up a little.

"What's the definition of...oh I don't know... Vmu?"

And guess what? Rattling around in my brain somewhere was the definition of Vmu, because I wrote it on my study guide and I'd been re-reading that thing for the last couple of weeks. So, I gave him the answer and I could tell he was pleased.

I'd been combing through the gouge for weeks and I never once saw Vmu mentioned. The guy asking the question knew Vmu wasn't out there, because he knows what's on the gouge, too. You can't answer unexpected questions if you prepare with nothing more than rote memorization. He asked me something outside what was

149

expected, and I had an answer for him. Welcome to new-hire training.

Let's work through a more complex example. You've broken your questions down into subject areas, and the company you're interviewing with focuses a lot on instrument procedures.

One question under your subject area *Instrument Procedures* is, "When can you descend below decision height?"

You *think* you know the answer: When you get the runway environment in sight. That's what you remember your instrument flight instructor told you, anyway. But you think there may be more to it than that. So you look it up.

The question seems like something that would be covered by a regulation, so you go to FAR part 121, air carrier operations. Look through the table of contents for regulations that seem applicable. Eventually, and it probably won't be your first stop, you'll get to FAR 121.651. Oh, and look, there are actually a whole slew of things you need to go below decision height. Copy all these items next to the question that started you on this quest, along with the reference 121.651. You end up with the raw regulation that looks like this:

The pilot may continue the approach below DA/DH or MDA if either the requirements of 91.175(l) of this chapter, or the following requirements are met:
(1) The aircraft is continuously in a position from which a descent to a landing on the intended runway can be made at a normal rate of descent using normal maneuvers, and

150

where that descent rate will allow touchdown to occur within the touchdown zone of the runway of intended landing;

(2) The flight visibility is not less than the visibility prescribed in the standard instrument approach procedure being used;

(3) Except for Category II or Category III approaches where any necessary visual reference requirements are specified by authorization of the Administrator, at least one of the following visual references for the intended runway is distinctly visible and identifiable to the pilot:

(i) The approach light system, except that the pilot may not descend below 100 feet above the touchdown zone elevation using the approach lights as a reference unless the red terminating bars or the red side row bars are also distinctly visible and identifiable.

(ii) The threshold.

(iii) The threshold markings.

(iv) The threshold lights.

(v) The runway end identifier lights.

(vi) The visual approach slope indicator.

(vii) The touchdown zone or touchdown zone markings.

(viii) The touchdown zone lights.

(ix) The runway or runway markings.

(x) The runway lights.

Now you've got *a regulation* that you know for a fact gets hit on in the interview, not just one question *about* the regulation. Instead of just learning the answer to the question that brought you here, you need to learn the regulation, and be able to apply it. Regulations do not come in an easy-to-study format. Reading through the regulation, we can boil down the most important elements into terms we can understand.

I can descend below decision height under the following circumstances:

1. Using normal descent rates and maneuvers to land in the touchdown zone.
2. The flight visibility is not less than that prescribed in the approach.
3. Having one of the following in sight:
   a. Approach lights, but only to 100' above touchdown zone *unless* the red terminating bars or red side row bars are also visible.
   b. Touchdown zone, lights or markings.
   c. Runway, lights or markings.
   d. Threshold, lights or markings.
   e. Runway end identifier lights (REILS).
   f. Visual approach slope indicator (VASI).

Now that you've boiled it down, you need a way to remember it in an interview. A lot of people like acronyms. Assign a letter to each item you need to remember and make a word out of it to jog your memory.

My personal method is to write out the study guide by hand. It takes longer than cutting and pasting, especially when you have to force yourself to write neatly, but the extra time and effort is worthwhile. I've found that after handwriting something and then studying it over and over again, I can picture the study sheet in my head. When an applicable question comes up in the interview, I mentally picture the study sheet and read it from the picture in my mind.

Whatever method you use for remembering laundry lists of information in aviation (and I'm sure you have your own by now), apply it. Researching interview questions this way may initially seem like a lot of work, but it goes quicker than you might first think. Each piece of knowledge will build on the next, until you have a rock-solid foundation to build your answers. Knowing information, instead of memorizing rote answers to questions, gives you the ability to apply knowledge and make good decisions. That's what they want to see in the interview.

The gouge question we started with was, "When can you descend below decision height?"

When you get to your interview, the question may change to something like, "If you have the approach lights in sight, how low can you descend?"

Same subject matter, completely different question.

Since you've done the work and learned the reason *behind* the answer, you can apply that knowledge. With only the approach lights in sight, you can descend to 100' above touchdown zone elevation, unless you also have the red terminating bars or the red side row bars in sight. What exactly *are* red terminating bars and red side row bars? If you read a term you're not familiar with, look it up. See how the whole process works?

As your knowledge base grows, you will get more efficient at finding and organizing information. When your interviewers change their questions slightly, which they can and will do, you'll be ready. You will have an understanding of how to *apply* knowledge, instead of only having specific answers to specific questions.

What to do when you just don't know

At some point, a technical question will come up in your interview and you will not know the answer. It's almost inevitable. There's nothing wrong with not knowing *an* answer. If you only know 1 out of 5 answers, that will be a problem. Coming across issues you're not familiar with happens in real life. Inevitably, you will someday be faced with a question you don't know the answer to. Dealing effectively with the unexpected is what makes a good pilot. Your interviewers will be paying careful attention to how you react to the unexpected, and there are right and wrong ways to deal with not knowing an answer.

Saying, "I don't know," and giving up on a question is *not* what you want to do in the interview. If you're the captain of an airplane, you can never just give up and hope things will work themselves out. You must come up with *an* answer, even if it's not the best *possible* answer.

When a stumper comes up and you go totally blank, you need to give your interviewers some kind of resolution. Fall back on your current operational experience and explain how you would deal with it there.

Here's another personal example:

I was interviewing with a US Legacy carrier, and they asked me what color type IV de-ice fluid was. When I tried to access that information, my brain simply laughed at me. It was there somewhere, rattling around, I just wasn't going to get it in a timely manner. I responded that I'd never used type IV; I'd only used type I. I told them what color type I was. I then explained that the types and colors of all fluids were listed in our

155

POH under de-icing operations, and if I found myself in a situation where we were receiving type IV fluid, I would be referencing those pages beforehand. They thought that was good enough and moved on.

Not the right answer, necessarily, but that's how you handle the unexpected in real life. There is so much information out there in so many areas it's impossible to know everything, at least for me anyway. Describing how you would deal with the unexpected or unknown is usually an acceptable alternative.

There are two things you need to remember about this method:

1. You can only use it once or twice at the most. If you tell them you have to reference every question they ask you, that doesn't look very good.

2. If you're stumped on a procedural question, where you wouldn't realistically *have* time to look something up (what would you do at this point on the approach if you lost radio communications), you have to pick the safest course of action and just take a shot. If it's wrong, it's wrong, but make the best decision you can with regard to safety. Remember, *a* decision is better than *no* decision.

Your interviewers are looking to hire captains, not career first officers. They need a person who will make the best decision they can under the given conditions. Giving an answer, even if it's not the right answer, sends a much stronger impression than no answer at all. Don't ever throw up your hands and just give up. No one wants to be onboard that person's airplane.

Technical interview summary

You want your answers to technical questions to be short, sweet, and correct. Most technical questions can be answered with just a few words, and you should try to be as efficient in your answers as possible.

If you're asked, "What's the definition of V1?"

Your answer should be, "Takeoff safety speed."

Don't give long, rambling answers to technical questions. That's the point of the technical portion of the interview. You either know the answer or you don't. The longer your answer, the greater the chance you'll say something that gives the impression you're not sure about what you're saying. If they want more, they'll ask.

Finally, and you may be getting sick of hearing this, *practice*. Once you have an interview study sheet from the gouge completed and organized, practice verbalizing your answers to the applicable subjects. Actually getting the answers to come out of your mouth is different from going through it all in your head. If you don't practice the physical act of verbalizing answers, I guarantee you your answers won't sound as good in real life as they do in your head. I've had some fantastic conceptual answers in my mind that somehow turned into gibberish when I tried to get them out. Have someone read questions to you while you actually speak your answers. If you can't beg or bribe anyone to help, go through questions yourself. Just do it out loud. While talking to yourself may be frowned upon in some circles, it's OK in this case. This won't be the first or last time you'll seem crazy because you've gotten into aviation.

Don't restrict yourself to only answering questions from the gouge. Come up with your own questions based on the subject areas you're focusing on.

"I see a lot of questions about mach tuck and Dutch roll. What other types of aerodynamics questions could I be asked?"

157

If you can't think of any follow up questions, you don't know the subject area well enough.

The technical portion of the interview is your chance to really impress your interviewers. Nothing sends a better impression of competence and capability than a strong display of technical knowledge. While it may seem there is an insurmountable amount of information, research and preparation will help effectively focus your efforts. Maintaining a high level of proficiency at your current job will help when you start interview preparation. You'll already have a good portion of the information down. Be thorough and diligent in your preparation and it will pay off in the end.

Here's the final lifeline: If you come across a question or concept you cannot answer or don't understand *how* to answer, send me an email (rick@airline-career.net) and we'll work it out together.

Points to remember

✓ Study your current operation and aircraft like you would for a check ride, starting now. You will get questions about your current operations, and you will fall back on this knowledge when you can't think of the exact answer they're asking for.

✓ Break down the interview gouge by question into subject areas. Create an interview study sheet where you compile all the information for the applicable subject areas in an easy to study format. Use acronyms or some other memory aid to help remember study items with multiple elements.

✓ As you research the subject areas, *don't glance over* terms or concepts you are not familiar with. Follow up on that term or concept until you understand it.

- ✓ Answer technical questions as clearly and directly as possible. Don't give long, vague answers that will lead to more questions. Use the least amount of words possible to fully answer the question, and then stop.
- ✓ Listen carefully to each question. Make sure you answer the question they are asking to the best of your capabilities.
- ✓ Don't ever say, "I don't know" in an interview and leave it at that. *An* answer is better than *no* answer, even if it's not correct. Refer back to your current experience and operation and explain how you would find the information if you needed it in real life.
- ✓ Practice verbalizing your answers.

Part 6

The subjective interview

ubjective interview questions should be handled
differently from technical ones. Take your time and
think your answers through. You don't get any points
for speed in this round.

The question was old, and had been around for a long time on the gouge. I still liked to ask it, however, because it will always be a complex issue.

"You're shooting an ILS approach and the captain is the pilot flying. The autopilot is on. You get to minimums and don't see anything. You call out, 'Go Around.' The captain does nothing, and the aircraft continues descending below minimums, with no runway in sight. What would you do?"

The applicant was obviously ready for this question. As I said, it was old and had been reprinted on the gouge a million times. I knew he had prepared for this one specifically because there was absolutely no hesitation before his answer.

"I would say three times, 'Captain, we're below minimums.' Then I would raise the landing gear."

Imagine the screeching metal on metal sound a freight train makes when it suddenly applies maximum braking, sending off showers of glowing sparks and billowing smoke as it grinds to an earsplitting halt on the tracks. That's what happened in my head when I heard this answer.

I had to really consider this course of action for a moment before proceeding. I'd read about a very similar answer to this one on some gouge a couple of weeks ago. When I read it at the time, I thought it was a really bad idea. Now that I heard someone giving the answer in real life, it sounded even worse. I imagined a planeload full of people barreling toward a runway at 150mph that the pilots couldn't see, and this person's solution to that impending problem was to raise the landing gear. Didn't seem very well thought out.

I don't know for sure he got this answer from the gouge, but I'm making the assumption someone at some point told him this was the thing to do. Once you throw your answer out there for everyone in an interview setting, you own it. Good idea or not.

This is a great example of why you don't want YOUR answers to be influenced by someone else's bad idea just because they posted it online or told you their friend's cousin's uncle got hired at Delta and this is what he said.

"Okay," I responded after getting my head around the situation. "Why is raising the landing gear when you're less than 200 feet above the ground and descending the best course of action here?"

"It would force the captain to go around," he said very confidently.

Now it became a little clearer. He was making an assumption about the question I was asking. He assumed the captain was going below minimums on purpose. The question he was answering wasn't actually the one I was asking.

"What if the captain wasn't intentionally going below minimums but was incapacitated? Maybe he or she quietly had a stroke. Would raising the landing gear still be the best course of action?"

"Oh. I thought he was doing it on purpose. I guess I would do something different then if that was the situation."

I purposely didn't ask a follow up question. I wanted to see if he'd take the initiative, think it through, and clarify his position.

After about 15 seconds of dead air time, I was still waiting and he hadn't specified what "something different" was. We were just sitting there, uncomfortably staring at each other. I moved on, the screeching freight train sound reverberating in my ears. This applicant left me with the impression of a planeload of people crashing onto the runway because he hadn't thought the situation through. This applicant had a canned answer to a question he thought he would get. Unfortunately, it wasn't a very good or well thought out answer.

Interview Train Wreck #16

I was observing a new interviewer before signing him off to conduct interviews on his own. The applicant he was interviewing had a pretty good amount of flight time. He was currently a 727 flight engineer for a shady cargo outfit.

(A flight engi-what?! On REALLY OLD airplanes, a third pilot managed the aircraft systems while the captain and first officer flew the airplane. C'mon, it wasn't THAT long ago...)

162

The applicant had done OK in the sim (minimum standard but definitely not dazzling) and was about 70/30 for technical questions. I personally was on the fence about him; everything was meeting the minimums, but just barely. I wasn't sure what the interviewer asking the questions was thinking, however, and I was going to leave the final decision up to him.

"Tell me about a time you made a mistake in the cockpit," the interviewer asked.

The applicant thought for a second, and then began, "I had a runway incursion one night in the 72. It was real late, we were taxiing out, and the captain thought we were cleared into position on the runway. I wasn't really watching where we were going because I was so tired, I was just staring at the panel. When we got to the hold short line, the captain taxied right past it and lined up on the runway without stopping. Tower came on the radio and asked why we'd taxied onto the runway when we were only cleared to the hold short line."

"The FO got on the radio and said, 'Sorry, we thought we were cleared onto the runway.' Tower replied, 'Don't worry about it; there's no other traffic on the field. Just listen up next time.'

"That was probably my biggest mistake," the applicant concluded.

I quickly glanced through his paperwork and saw he didn't claim to have any accidents, incidents, or violations. I needed a little clarification.

"Did the tower report it?" I asked.

"I don't think so," the applicant said. "We never heard anything more about it."

First, I had to give the guy points for being truthful. Second, I would never fault anyone for an honest mistake. I've made my fair share. Probably more than my fair share, if I totaled them all up.

What I could fault him for was:

- *Using really poor judgment in his choice of a past experience to bring up. The question is "Tell us about a mistake," not "Tell us about your worst mistake ever."*
- *Not following up with how this mistake made him a better pilot. You can make a mistake. You can even make a BIG mistake. You should ALWAYS follow up with what you've learned and how you've changed your behavior so it won't happen again.*
- *Putting us, as interviewers, in a corner. Say we hire him, and he has another runway incursion, only this time there is some traffic out there and people get hurt or worse. Now it comes back to us because we knew he had a history, but hired him anyway.*

Runway incursions are a REALLY, REALLY BIG DEAL. The deadliest accident in aviation history was due to two 747s colliding on a runway, Pan Am 1736 and KLM 4805 in Tenerife.

People make mistakes. Runway incursions happen without costing lives, and you can absolutely get hired somewhere if you have a runway incursion on your record, BUT your interview is NOT the place to bear all your sins, ESPECIALLY sins there are no official record of. Your interview is the time to emphasize how great and competent and safe you are. Note: I'm not saying to lie about anything, just use sound judgment in what YOU choose to bring up.

The biggest part to being effective in a subjective interview is knowing which experiences to talk about and which skeletons to leave in your closet.

After the interview was over and the applicant was gone, the other interviewer and I discussed it. He was of the opinion the applicant's overall performance was marginal, but the runway incursion story had pushed him over the top. He didn't want to recommend the applicant. I said the decision was his, but I also agreed with him.

The lasting impression this applicant left me with was of him nodding off late at night while the captain taxied in front of a landing aircraft. Boom, screaming death and destruction, and it all gets laid at my feet because I hired him. I couldn't do it.

I've lumped all questions that aren't technical into the Subjective Questions category. They'll get broken into some sub-categories momentarily, but for right now, what do I mean by Subjective Questions? A Subjective Question is one that doesn't have a right or wrong answer.

For pilots in particular, subjective questions are some of the hardest to deal with. We like answers in black and white, not shades of gray.

"The visibility is a ¼ mile, can you start the approach?"

That's easy, you either can or you can't.

What's the right answer to, "Why should we hire you?"

Is there one? It totally depends on your interviewer's interpretation of your answer. That's the hard part about these questions. The perceptions of right and wrong are based on opinion. You need to figure out what your interviewers want to see, and show them you possess the qualities they're looking for through your answers. The "right" way to answer these questions is to leave no doubt in your interviewers' minds you are the person they should hire. The "wrong" way is to leave them wondering if you could fly your way out of a paper bag.

Every answer you give to every Subjective Question is a chance to sell yourself and the qualities you will bring to the company. All you need to do is make sure you're selling something they want.

You need to study for subjective questions just like you would technical questions. When you created your study guide for technical questions, you separated any that didn't have a right or wrong answer. Now, look at the subjective questions. What do they focus on? Are they operational scenarios? What would you do if...? Tell me about a time...? Group these questions together just like you did with the technical ones. Some airlines focus mainly on how you would handle situations in the airplane. Others want to know how you interact with people. And yet others incorporate a little bit of everything. Know what areas your interviewers will focus on and emphasize them in your preparation.

Practice speaking your answers to Subjective Questions the same way you do for Technical Questions, with one important difference: subjective answers are not technical answers, and will require some forethought. Technical answers have a right or wrong answer. Subjective answers require you to relate an experience or thought process. Snapping technical answers back looks great, feels great, and is great. If you start trying to snap subjective answers back, something will come out of your mouth that will make the voice inside your head scream, "*Oh my God, did I really just say that*?" But you've already said it, and once it's out there you can't take it back.

How do you avoid throwing a live hand grenade into the interview room? When you are asked a subjective question, sit back, look up, and take a few seconds to collect your thoughts. It's not a race. You don't get points for starting your answer as quickly as possible. You do get points for a well thought out, well-spoken answer. Get everything straight in your head for about 3 to 5 seconds before you start verbalizing. Try practicing your answers both ways, with and without a pause, to see the difference. You'll find that a little forethought goes a long, long way in subjective answers.

What do they want to hear?

We said different companies have different personalities. Does one company want one thing in their pilots, while another wants something else? Not really, they just go about it in different ways. Companies want to hire future captains who will produce the best possible results over the course of their employment. They want people who will do a good job, enjoy doing it, and get along with those around them while they're doing it. There are the four *core* qualities any company wants to see in a pilot:

1. Safe
2. Legal
3. Efficient
4. Compatible

Four qualities. Doesn't seem that bad, does it? What you need to demonstrate through your answers, *every single* answer that you give, is that you embody these qualities. Every answer you come up with should revolve around them. If they ask you what animal you would be (don't laugh, I've actually gotten that) you need to think about which animal embodies these four qualities. Elephant was the answer I gave. It seemed to fit the mold, plus I just like elephants (whatever that means, Sigmund Freud...). Was it the right answer to the question? Who knows? The question and answer are totally subjective.

What do I mean by Safe, Legal, Efficient, and Compatible? In the words of the great M.C. Hammer, let's break it down:

Safe: Airlines that crash a lot don't do very well financially, which is undesirable from an employer's standpoint. Plus, someone in the interview room, or their family, may be on your flight someday. No one in that room can have any reservations about getting on your aircraft after they meet you. You need to impress on them safety is your priority. You're most likely interviewing for a First Officer position, but someday you'll be a Captain. Your interviewers have to be able to picture you in BOTH capacities. They don't want career Second Officers, or Relief Pilots, or First Officers. They want an applicant who will be a good new-hire First Officer *and* a good Captain someday.

Let's talk about your role at any given company for a minute. Assuming you're hired as a pilot, what's your primary responsibility? Fly the airplane? Assist the captain? Do the walk-around when it's raining? Sure, the job includes all those elements and many others.

Your primary job, as a flight crewmember in *any* capacity, is to *ensure the safety of each flight.* When you're hired, you will have a lot of different duties and areas of responsibility. They are all secondary to ensuring the safety of the flight. Safety of flight is your most important job and you have to prove to your interviewers that you understand this. How do you prove you're safe? By demonstrating it in everything you do on interview day. A proficient pilot is a safe pilot, demonstrated in the simulator. A technically knowledgeable pilot is a safe pilot. A pilot who pays attention to detail (paperwork, paperwork, paperwork) is a safe pilot. And finally, a pilot who factors safety into every decision they make is a safe pilot. Emphasize this quality in your decision-making and show your interviewers that safety of flight is always at the forefront of your thinking.

Legal: You need to demonstrate your commitment to maintaining the legality of the operation. Safe operations are great. Safe and legal are even better. In order to show your interviewers you consider the legal aspects of your decisions, you first need to know what they are. Knowing what's legal and what's not goes back to being prepared. You can't make sound decisions and demonstrate your commitment to legality if you're not sure what the legal decision really is. Know what's legal, and show your interviewers it's a high priority for you.

Efficient: While it's true most companies exist solely to provide you with an airplane to fly, they may mistakenly view themselves as businesses trying to turn a profit. After you consider the safety and legal aspects of any decisions, you need to factor in the business side. Safe operations are great. Safe and legal are even better. Making a decision that considers safety, legality, and efficiency is the best possible operational decision you can make.

Unfortunately, safety and legality don't always go hand in hand with efficiency. In your interview questions, they will most likely be in direct conflict. After considering safety and legality, demonstrate you can and will conduct operations efficiently. The company wants someone who will be a good employee, and ultimately make them money.

"I need to divert for this malfunction. Should I go to this airport in the middle of nowhere, or that airport that's a little farther away but has a maintenance base?"

Depends on the malfunction. Does it compromise safety to go to the maintenance base? If it doesn't, is the maintenance base airport legal? If both choices are safe and legal, then make the best *operational* decision.

Your interviewers want someone who will factor in the best interests of the company. Efficiency, schedule integrity, good customer service, and a million other business considerations all contribute to the company's bottom line. The people conducting your interview depend on the company's bottom line, and they want someone who will contribute. Your operational decisions affect them directly. You can run the safest and most legally compliant airline in the world, but if the company doesn't make any money, you'll be bragging about that safety record to the other guys living in vans down by the river.

Compatible: Being compatible is listed as number 4, but it's a special case. You can be safe, you can be legal, and you can be efficient, but if you're a raging a-hole, you're not going to be a good addition to the team. You need to demonstrate compatibility in everything you do, and in every decision that you make.

There's never a good time to come across as hard to deal with. You need to show compatibility with everyone around you *while* you balance safety, legality, and efficiency. You need to demonstrate that you can work effectively with anyone, even if they *are* hard to deal with.

HR representatives are wondering if you'll be a good fit for the corporate culture. They are trying to establish how you'll get along with other pilots, passengers, ground service personnel, crew scheduling, etc.

The pilot side of the equation is continually wondering, "Do I want to be locked in a cockpit on a week-long trip with this person?"

I've said before that airlines are like people; they each have a different personality. I have yet to find a company, however, that doesn't want people who are easy to get along with. This is an important trait to demonstrate in your overall presentation.

Points to remember

✓   There are four qualities you must show your interviewers you possess. You must demonstrate them throughout all of your of answers and actions. The first three qualities are being safe, legal, and efficient, in that order. The final quality you need to present, at *all* times, is being compatible.

Subjective questions

Subjective questions can be further sub-divided into two categories: Human Resource and situational questions. Let's talk about the Human Resource category first.

These are getting-to-know-you type questions. They don't necessarily have anything directly to do with being a pilot specifically, but are aimed more at finding out what makes you tick as an individual. They tend to focus on your thoughts, feelings, motivations, and background, etc. This part of the interview is really just like sitting down and having a conversation about you.

A lot of people don't like talking about themselves, and because of that tend to be overly brief and not make a big deal of their accomplishments. If you fall into this category (and I actually do, despite all the personal back-patting you're reading here), you'll have to get over it. Talking about yourself is your opportunity to show them what a great person you are. You can (and should) be humble, but don't miss this opportunity to show them what an asset you can be to their operation.

For preparation, focus on the questions from your study sheet that don't have anything specific to do with flying. These are your HR questions. You will see they're both general and non-specific. In addition to what you get from the gouge, come up with some of your own. Just Google "HR Questions" and you'll get more examples than you can realistically work through. Anything that could reasonably be asked in an interview is fair game. Practicing general HR questions, even if they're not questions you'll necessarily get, will help you with your overall composition and delivery.

The following are important things to consider as you practice your Human Resource answers:

Don't script answers: When an applicant's eyes glaze over and they start giving a long monotone dialogue, you can just see them reading from the memorized script in their head. This doesn't mean you don't want to have something *general* in mind, however. Think of preparing for these questions by creating an outline, rather than a script. Know what important points you want to bring up, but don't memorize exactly how you want to say it. Also, with an outline instead of a script, you can work these important points into an answer for a whole array of questions, rather than one specifically.

Practice talking: Thinking and talking are two different things. If all you ever do is go through your answers in your head, they won't sound the same when they come out of your mouth. After spending some time actually verbalizing your answers, you'll find they come easier and flow better the more you do it. Always use a conversational tone: as if you were sitting in a coffee shop talking to some people you'd just met. Work on not giving rambling answers. You'll want to keep your answers less than 2 minutes long at the *absolute* most. Anything more than that and you'll start sounding like Charlie Brown's teacher to your interviewers. If you're not familiar with that reference, you can check it out on YouTube and you'll immediately see what I mean.

These questions you can count on

I know I keep saying not to script any answers or prepare for specific questions, and I stand by that. There are some Human Resource concepts, however, that you can safely bet money will be covered. You should get this information together, commit it to memory, and wait for the right time to bring it up, because it will come up.

<u>Know your history</u>: You *will always* get a question about your background. Be able to give a synopsis of your career up to the point where you're sitting in the interview chair. Focus on the highlights, and mention anything in your past that demonstrates safe, legal, efficient and compatible. Picture this as giving a verbal and slightly more detailed summary of your résumé, adding anything important that isn't listed there.

<u>Know about the company</u>: You *will always* get questions about the company and what you know about it. You should have the following facts and numbers committed to memory. The majority of this information is usually available on the company's own website. If not, you can find it with a minimal amount of research:

1. Know who's who. Have the names of the CEO, COO, and the Director of Flight Operations. The people conducting your interview answer to these executives directly in some cases. Show them you know who's running the company you want to be a part of.
2. Make notes of the company's history and key dates. Every company has a unique story about how it came to be. Know it. Specifically know when it was started and any major milestones.

3. Know the aircraft. You're trying to get a job flying their planes. Make sure you know what kind and how many planes they have. If the company is currently taking delivery of new aircraft (which, if you're interviewing, they may be) know the details of the aircraft to be acquired.

4. Know where the pilot bases are located. I asked an applicant once where he wanted to be based, and he said Salt Lake City. That was great except for the fact that we didn't have a base in Salt Lake City.

5. Significant press releases. Anything that directly affects flight operations is good to know going in.

6. The company's financial performance. Even if you're interviewing someplace that's lost more money than a small country's Gross Domestic Product, you still need to show them you know how the company is performing financially. Knowing the company's profit/loss for the last several years is sufficient.

7. Know how the company views itself. Every airline has some type of vision statement or guiding principle they operate under. This is a great quotation to have and be able to bring up in an interview.

Strengths and weaknesses: You *will always* get a question related to these in some way. "What can you bring to the company?" "What are your best qualities?" "Why should we hire you?" Each of these questions and their many variations can easily be answered if you know what you're good at. Think of 4 or 5 qualities and some examples. Talking about your strengths is a great place to emphasize how much emphasis you place on safety, legality, and efficiency.

You'll also need to come up with one fault or weakness. Once you decide on something, also think of a way you are working to improve upon it. Try to come up with a *personal* fault, not necessarily a *professional* one. For example: it's better to say you keep a messy house rather than you have weak instrument flying skills. Failing to fulfill your goal of completing an ironman triathlon is better than saying you have a hard time working with others because they're stupid. Use some common sense when coming up with your weaknesses, and don't pick anything that says you're not safe, legal, and efficient.

Sell yourself: There is an old tried and proven sales technique that says at the end of your sales pitch, ask for the business. Whether you're selling a car, or trying to manage someone's retirement fund, you generally won't get the business if you don't ask for it.

This entire interview process is one big sales pitch. You are pitching yourself. At the end of the whole ordeal, ask for the job. It shows them how much you want to be a part of this company.

Your interview will almost always conclude with them asking if you have questions or anything you'd like to add. This is your opportunity to ask for the job. I know I've said over and over not to script answers, but there's an exception to every rule. You want to have a statement you can close the interview with, and it's good to think that one through beforehand.

It can be as simple as, "Thank you for the opportunity to come in and interview. I really hope I can be part of this company."

Your closing statement can be that simple, or it can be a more complex description about why this is the company you want to fly for. I don't want to give you too much direction, because it should come from you and be in your words. Just have a statement that thanks them and clearly states that you want the job. They may not give you something if you don't ask for it.

Points to remember

✓ Human resource questions are the way interviewers try to get to know the real person you are, outside of the cockpit. Don't script answers to these questions, but have an outline in your head to work from. You can virtually guarantee a few subject areas that will be covered in this section; make sure you prepare specifically for them. Have a good closing statement planned, and don't forget to *ask* for the job.

Situational questions

These are the second type of subjective questions you can and will be asked. Not all companies incorporate a straightforward technical interview. They don't ask you straight out when you can descend below minimums, because the right situational questions require you to incorporate technical knowledge and decision making into your answer all at once.

There are essentially two types of situational questions: Tell me about a time (TMAAT), and what would you do (WWYD). TMAAT are actual experiences that you have dealt with in your past. WWYD are theoretical scenarios you must work through. You will answer TMAAT questions by choosing real-life experiences that clearly demonstrate how you apply safety, legality, and efficiency. You will answer WWYD by employing a conflict resolution strategy and demonstrating how the 4 core qualities influence your decision-making in a theoretical situation.

TMAAT Questions: Answering a TMAAT question is essentially telling a story. You are relating a real-life experience from your past. Your story should be clear, and easy to understand. Don't assume that because you're a captain right now, your interviewers will know when the story you're telling took place. Don't assume your interviewers know anything about the story except what you tell them.

When telling TMAAT stories, you need a framework to relate the story that ensures the interviewers get all the information they need. Use the phrase *Situation/Action/Response* to help yourself construct your story effectively.

Here's how it works for the example question, "Tell me about a time you dealt with a conflict in the cockpit":

1. **Situation:** Provide the setup and background for the story. Don't assume your interviewers know at what point in your career this incident took place. You must provide the context. *"I was a first officer on the EMB-120 for XYZ airlines. We were setting up for the ILS approach into BFE airport and I was the pilot flying. It was the middle of the night..."*

2. **Action:** This is where your narrative starts. Give a clear explanation of the situation and exactly what happened and why it's applicable: *"The tower was closed and we were talking to a center controller, outside of radar contact. The captain was concerned we were getting high, so he told me to descend down to published approach altitude right away. I responded that we hadn't been cleared for the approach and couldn't descend, yet. He said we were cleared and to descend now. I asked him to clarify with ATC."*

3. **Response:** What happened. How was the situation resolved? Make sure you take the story all the way to the end. If I didn't fully conclude the story above, it would have ended with, "I asked him to clarify with ATC." Then the interviewers would have to draw their own conclusion. Who was right? Were we in fact cleared for the approach? Did the captain get bent out of shape? Did the aircraft make it onto the ground uneventfully? Make sure you take your story all the way to its final conclusion, and don't leave anything open for interpretation. *"The captain asked ATC if we were cleared for the approach. ATC said not yet, there was traffic crossing below. Shortly thereafter, they did clear us to descend and we made an uneventful approach and*

landing. After we shut down at the gate, the captain thanked me for making him verify our clearance and apologized."

The way to prepare for TMAAT questions is to spend some time thinking about your past experiences. A great time to do this is when you're working on your logbook. Certain entries will jog your memory. When something comes to mind that you think is a good story for an interview, write it down on your study guide or in a notebook. When an experience comes to mind that makes you cringe about how you handled it, that's a good one to leave at home.

Have as many good examples of stories from your past as you can. You'll probably use 4 or 5 of them, depending on the company and the type of interview.

The experiences you choose should say, "Look at how well I handled this situation; this is why you want to hire me."

Each experience you write down should clearly display safety, legality, and efficiency, in that order. Practice telling your stories. Practice using one good story to answer different variations of questions. If you have one great go-to story, it can be used for many different questions, but you'll want to have more than just that one. You can't keep referring back to the same example over and over.

Here is a list of the type of experiences you'll need at the minimum, going into the interview:

1. One thing you've done professionally so far that you are most proud of. The best decision you made, the most serious emergency you dealt with, the day your uniform looked the best, whatever. This example should be what you consider the highlight of your career performance up to this point.

2. Two experiences that deal with conflict resolution; one inside the cockpit and one outside the cockpit. Any type of conflict you resolved will do. A conflict can be as simple as a disagreement about what altitude you were cleared to maintain. Every conflict *does not* have to be a major safety issue or result in a knock-down drag-out fistfight. In fact, think the smaller the better. You obviously want these to be conflict resolutions you were *right* about and that you feel you handled well.

3. A time you went out of your way, above and beyond, or just showed some initiative to solve a problem.

4. An example of when you had to deal with something that wasn't covered by a checklist. A time you had to think outside the box.

5. In addition to the positive examples, you will need to come up with one experience that you *didn't* handle as well as you would have liked, but that you can put a *positive* spin on in the end. It can be a wrong decision, a mistake, or just something you regret doing the way you did, but conclude with what you learned and how it made you a better pilot/person. *Don't* pick the *worst* mistake you ever made in your life. It should be something small, but relevant. Explain the mistake and then make sure to conclude this experience with how it made you a better pilot/employee/person.

The experiences listed above will cover the majority of TMAAT interview questions. Use the gouge to see what specific areas a particular company likes to focus on, and think of personal stories that apply. One particular company asks a lot of variations on the question of whether or not you've broken rules or seen anyone who's broken rules. That's a line of questioning specific to this company's interview. If you're getting ready for an interview at this company, you'll want to have an applicable outline of an answer on your study sheet and in your head.

The TMAAT story example

Let's put it all together. Here's an example of one experience I always bring with me to an interview for TMAAT questions:

[SITUATION] *I was a captain on the CRJ and the pilot flying. I was flying with a First Officer who was much older than me, and he'd given me a few hints over the course of the trip that he resented that fact. We were doing a visual approach into Atlanta late one afternoon. It had been a long day and this was the last of our 5 legs. I had been watching what would soon be a thunderstorm building right over the top of the airport the entire way in on the arrival. It wasn't affecting the arrivals as of yet, and I hoped we would get on the ground before it did.*

[ACTION] *We were on final approach for Runway 25 Left, following a Delta MD-88. I could see the rain shaft from the building storm now hitting the airport. I knew we probably didn't have much longer before things got ugly. Landing aircraft ahead were reporting relatively calm winds, but I could hear from the reports the wind was building slightly with each arrival. The Delta flight right in front of us landed and reported winds 10 gusting to 15. That was well within our limits, but I couldn't shake this feeling that things just weren't right. The hairs were standing up on the back of my neck and my stomach was starting to do this gurgle-thing. My policy is "if something doesn't feel right, then it's probably not." That's exactly the feeling I was getting.*

I asked the First Officer to tell approach we were breaking off and needed a turn to the left, away from the weather.

He pointed out the window at the runway and said that he could see it right there; Delta got in just fine, and he wanted to continue.

I said I didn't feel good about it and calmly told him to ask approach control for the left turn.

He glared at me and made it clear through the tone of his radio transmission to approach that he disapproved of the decision.

Approach control came on the radio, and I could tell by the tone of his voice that breaking us out of the line of approaching aircraft was a major inconvenience to him as well.

Now I started wondering if I'd made the right decision. I was definitely upsetting everyone, all just because my stomach was gurgling. Once we finished our left turn, I realized I wasn't completely sure where we were going, since everyone behind us was continuing in to the runway. Was I going to be the only aircraft to divert? Do I get back in line and do the approach all over again? All this was going through my head when the approach controller came back on the radio and literally started yelling that there was a microburst alert and all approach clearances were cancelled. The aircraft immediately behind us reported severe turbulence on the go-around. The controller started giving rapid-fire instructions to all the aircraft behind us to avoid the weather that had now developed into a pretty severe thunderstorm. That microburst hit the runway at the exact time we would have been crossing the threshold.

[RESPONSE] We continued to get vectored around for another 20 minutes before I decided to divert to Chattanooga. We were followed shortly thereafter by many of the other aircraft that were being vectored around the weather in Atlanta. The storm over the field was so severe that all runways were closed for over an hour.

After the flight, the first officer said that breaking off the approach was a good decision. He apologized for second guessing me and admitted he was just thinking about getting home ASAP.

I learned that day to listen to my instincts if things don't seem right, no matter what everyone else around me says.

Notice I've deliberately left out quotations. In an interview, you want to avoid directly quoting people unless you have a very specific reason to do so. If you try to relate a conversation by quoting someone, and then quoting yourself, it comes out something like this:

"He said..."

"And then I said..."

"And then he was like..."

"And then I was like 'Oh no you didn't!'"

A better way to handle conversations in your stories is to describe what was said in general terms instead of trying to repeat every word that each participant said.

Why do I like this story? First, I think it does a good job demonstrating the priority I put on safety, legality, and efficiency. I think it also shows compatibility by demonstrating how I dealt with the pressure coming from the first officer against my decision.

1. **Safety:** I chose what I thought was the safest course of action given the circumstances. It would have been legal and more efficient to try and continue to Atlanta, but my safety concerns overrode those two factors.

2. **Legality:** I complied with all FARs and company policies over the course of the incident while maintaining the highest degree of safety.

3. **Efficiency:** Diverting doesn't usually help operational integrity. Diversions result in missed connections, lost bags, and generally upset passengers (similar issues on the cargo side). If your hands are tied, all you can do is try to mitigate the operational impact as much as possible. I considered the integrity of the operation by choosing to divert to Chattanooga, where we had company facilities available.

4. **Compatibility:** This story demonstrates how I deal with conflict in the cockpit. The FO didn't agree with my decision, but it didn't result in a cage fight.

Here's the reason you only need 4 or 5 good stories: If you pick good stories that demonstrate your core qualities, you can use them for any number of questions. How many questions could I use the above story for? By changing the wording or emphasizing certain parts of the story, I can use it in any number of different ways.

"Tell me about a time you had a conflict in the cockpit."

"Tell me about a situation you've dealt with that wasn't covered by a checklist."

"Tell me about a time you second-guessed a decision."

"Give me an example of your leadership style as a captain."

"Tell me about an unpopular decision you made."

"Tell me about a challenging flight."

Get the drift? I just picked these questions randomly from gouge for different airlines, and I can use this one story to answer all of them.

Choose your stories wisely. Interviewers place a lot of weight on how you've handled situations in the past; it is a great indicator for how you'll perform in the future. You've had experiences where you've made great decisions, as well as ones you'd probably like to forget all together. The trick to being effective in the TMAAT section of an interview is using good judgment in the stories you choose. The other trick is to practice relating your stories.

TMAAT answers that crater like lead balloons do so for two reasons:

1. Choosing the wrong story to tell.
2. A breakdown in the telling of the story.

How can you tell a good story if you're not a storyteller? Use the situation, action, response model to help you with the presentation and ensure your stories come out in a coherent manner. Tell the story like you would to a group of people who have no idea about flying.

When I practice putting these answers together, I imagine how I would explain them to my aunt. She doesn't know the difference between an ILS, GPS, EGPWS, or a 3GS. She hasn't quite accepted the fact that I actually fly an airplane for a living (or a pretend airplane, in the case of running the simulator). She will forever picture me as a small child running around in green Yoda pajamas with the footies attached. When I practice telling these stories, I break them down to the level that she would understand, because I can't count on her making any assumptions. Just like you don't want your interviewers to have to make any assumptions. Always give full explanations for the decisions you made, why you decided what you did, and why it was right.

Points to remember

✓ Use good judgment in choosing the stories you want to relate in your interview. Well-chosen stories can be used for a wide range of answers. Make sure you choose stories from your past that demonstrate safety, legality, efficiency, and compatibility.
✓ Use the situation, action, and response model to make sure your stories are structured in a coherent manner.
✓ When relating your stories, don't quote people directly unless there is a specific reason to do so. Relate conversations by *describing what was said*, not repeating both sides of the conversation.

WWYD questions

Hijackers storm the cockpit while your drunken captain is shutting down the wrong engine without looking at the checklist. What would you do?

WWYD questions are theoretical problem-solving exercises that are limited only by your interviewer's imaginations. The interviewers throw a situation in your lap and you verbally describe how you work through it while they observe your thought process. WWYD questions deal with solving a problem, making a decision, and/or resolving a conflict.

Like with the TMAAT questions, what are interviewers looking for with these types of questions? They want to see you have a solid method for making decisions, and they want to understand how you apply this method. I alluded to this earlier; having a solid decision-making framework is important for an interview, but it's even more important in real life. Making good decisions is an essential skill for a pilot. In order to consistently come up with good decisions, you need to have a framework that can deal with any problem.

There is an easy system you can use to ensure you arrive at the right decision every time. Guess what? It's directly related to the core qualities we've already discussed. The only difference is instead of demonstrating you have them, you now need to prioritize them.

The biggest difference in the two question formats is that with TMAAT, you choose the story. In WWYD, you must decide how to arrive at the best possible solution to a theoretical issue. Here's how to prioritize your core values:

1. **Safety:** Safety is always your primary goal. Always. Anytime you're faced with a decision-making problem, this is the first thing to consider. Ask yourself which

options are safe, and which are not. Example: *A situation/malfunction arises that forces you to divert. If the situation is serious, like a cargo fire, the safety of the flight is immediately affected. You can land anywhere. Legality and efficiency are not even considerations. The only consideration is to get the airplane on the ground* <u>*safely.*</u>

2. **Legality:** Your next consideration is legality. If safety is not compromised, what are your options that ensure you comply with all applicable regulations and procedures? The only time you <u>can</u> break the law is when the safety of the flight depends on it. Example: *A malfunction forces you to divert. If the malfunction is not affecting the safety of flight, you must choose a diversion airport that meets legal requirements. An airport where the company has maintenance facilities is below landing minimums, while another one with no maintenance is above minimums. Taking into consideration the nature of the malfunction, you could try to wait as long as your fuel will allow for the airport with maintenance, but ultimately you <u>cannot</u> break the law if safety is not a question. Even if someone really, really wants you to.*

3. **Efficiency:** After you're satisfied that safety and legality are taken care of, the final thing to consider is: *which decision is in the best interest of the company.* Pretend one of the company accountants is in the jumpseat behind you. Try to make the decision that would make the accountant the happiest. Example: *A malfunction forces you to divert. It's not affecting the safety of the flight and we have several airports to choose from that meet legal requirements. Call the company and see*

which airport would be the best operational choice from the passenger/cargo/maintenance perspective. If you can't call the company, try to make the best operational decision based on the information you have.

If you effectively apply the safety, legality, and efficiency framework, you will display the decision-making priorities your interviewers are looking for. What if you're interviewing somewhere and you're not exactly sure what their legal requirements are? This happened to me at an interview in Hong Kong. They gave me a long, complicated scenario involving fuel and legality.

"You're at such and such a point with such and such fuel and the weather in Hong Kong is such and such. What would you do?"

I had no idea what they were looking for. I didn't have a clue what the fuel requirements were for an airline based in Hong Kong. But I did know what the fuel requirements were for my current operation, good ole' US FAR part 121. I'd studied it until my eyes bled for just this type of situation (remember, always know your own operation and fall back on it in times of crisis).

I qualified my answer with, "I'm not sure how you do things here, but if I were faced with this situation in my current operation..." and then I applied the rules I was familiar with.

The answer I gave was that I would continue to Hong Kong, after which I gave a brief rundown on my current operational fuel requirements, and then summed up that continuing to planned destination was safe, legal (under my current rules), and the best operational decision.

I found out after I was employed there that while my answer was legal by FAR part 121, it was not legal by their regulations. In the interview I'd thoroughly explained how and why I'd arrived at my decision. The answer wasn't correct for their operations, but they were happy enough with the *process* I'd used to reach the decision. Applying the safety, legality, and efficiency rule will lead you to the best available solution every time. Honestly, this is how I make operational decisions every day in real life.

Resolving conflicts is another important aspect of WWYD questions. The same safety, legality, and efficiency method applies. There is an added dynamic, however, of convincing or dealing with another person who isn't on the same page as you, all while maintaining compatibility. You not only have to come up with a solution to the situation in question, but you have to figure out how to get the other crewmembers on board in the most non-confrontational way possible.

Here's the trick to effectively dealing with theoretical conflict in an interview:

1. Determine the best course of action. Again, prioritize safety, legality, and efficiency.

2. If the situation involves a conflict, state your position clearly and unemotionally. Give the supporting reasons for your decision. Depending on the specific situation, you may need to issue an ultimatum. The ultimatum is a warning of what you will be forced to do if the situation is not corrected.

3. Your ultimatum can be anything from filing a report to calling the chief pilot to taking the controls of the airplane. Choose the most *conservative* ultimatum that will still address the issue and conclude the situation. For example: If you're (theoretically) flying with a captain who does things his own way and is not using normal procedures, instead of saying you'd hit him over the head with the crash axe and take control, warn him that if he doesn't start

complying with procedures you'll both have to sit down with the chief pilot and discuss the situation. The more serious the situation (safety of the aircraft being compromised in flight is the most serious) the more serious your ultimatum.

4. Always bring the situation to its full and logical conclusion in your answer. You can summarize your answers with "under no circumstances would I allow the aircraft's safety or legality to be compromised."

The two impressions you *don't* want to give are that you're either too wishy-washy or too confrontational. As a wise man once said, "you want to take the middle path." Make a good decision, and then stick to it without getting confrontational.

1. Work your way up to acting on your ultimatum. Like climbing a set of stairs, you should have a first, second, and third step.

2. The first step is to give everyone the benefit of the doubt. Maybe they just don't fully understand what's going on. You don't want to start calling the chief pilot and grounding the flight if someone is making an honest mistake. Start off any conflict-resolution scenario by simply clarifying the situation. Example: *Captain, I understand you don't want to write up that inoperative item and delay the flight, but it's required equipment and we can't legally go without it.*

3. The next step is to verbally draw a line in the sand and clearly state what the available options are. Here, you're basically coming up with the ultimatum

you'll follow through with if the situation isn't corrected. The ultimatum should be an action that stops the scenario without escalating the conflict. Example: *We need to write up this item and get it fixed or deferred, or I'm not going to be able to operate this flight.*

4. The final step is to follow through with your ultimatum. You don't necessarily need to describe how you would follow through unless your interviewers keep pushing the scenario. They may say something like, "You say that, but the captain still won't write it up. It's the last leg and he wants to get home." At that point, you describe how you stop the scenario from continuing. Example: *I would call the chief pilot, or whoever my direct supervisor is in your operation, and explain the situation. I would let them know that I'm not comfortable operating a flight that isn't legally compliant, which is currently the case. As soon as we can get this situation taken care of, I'm happy to operate it.*

When you're dealing with WWYD questions, be calm, non-confrontational, and make good decisions. That's all you can do in real life, and it's all your interviewers want to see. At the end of the day, they want to watch your problem-solving method and make sure it will fit in with their culture. The best way to demonstrate that is to make good all-around decisions, both operationally and when dealing with people.

I know I keep harping on this, and I'm really not trying to just burn up pages, but the single most important thing you can do to prepare for subjective questions is to practice. And when I say practice, I mean sitting down and speaking out loud. When you first start working through subjective questions, getting your answers out is like pulling teeth, only slightly more painful. But, the more you do it, the easier it will get. After practicing for a few days, your answers will flow more naturally and you'll start to sound like you actually know what you're talking about.

During your practice, don't just focus on subjective questions that come up on the gouge. The thing about subjective questions is they can be about anything. Working on answers to new and unexpected questions will help you perform effectively when you actually get into the hot seat. Pick questions from gouge for other airlines at random. Come up with the most difficult question you can imagine and verbalize an answer to it. Think of your answers to subjective questions as sitting down and simply having a conversation about what you would do if faced with this situation. The more you practice, the more relaxed you'll be in the interview. The more relaxed you are, the better your conversation will be.

Points to remember

✓ When answering WWYD questions, always prioritize safety, legality, and efficiency to make the best decision you can.
✓ For confrontational scenarios, make a decision and stick to it. Come up with an ultimatum that's appropriate to the situation. Resolve the situation with the minimal amount of confrontation possible.

Subjective interview summary

It's tough answering questions that don't have right answers. That is why you have to keep in mind what your interviewers are trying to accomplish. They are listening to your answers, don't think they're not, but more importantly they're listening to *how* you come up with your answers. They're listening to why you made this decision or that decision, and what you learned from it. They may not necessarily even agree with a decision that you made in the past or hypothetically make in the interview, but all you need them to agree with is the manner in which you make decisions. Structure all your decision-making and all your stories by ranking safety, legality, and efficiency in that order. Show compatibility with others at all times.

Take your time coming up with your answers. Snapping back technical answers is great, but snapping back answers to questions that require careful consideration will get you into trouble. Give yourself a few seconds to breath, organize your thoughts, and then give your answers in a calm and conversational tone.

The subjective interview is your chance to sit around, tell stories, and talk about what-if. Luckily for you, since you are a pilot, you are genetically pre-programmed to want to tell stories and talk about flying. If you want to get the job, you absolutely must practice talking and telling your stories. At the very least, it will give you the opportunity to force someone to sit in one place while you regale them with tales of your greatness.

At the end of the day, be yourself

There's been a lot of: "Do this! Act this way! Say this, but don't say that!" In giving you all the suggestions I have and relating my personal experiences and what I've witnessed over the years, there is one important message that I want to make clear: In any interview setting, regardless of the specific job, always be yourself. If you are taking the time to read this book in an effort to do the best you possibly can, you already *are* the person employers are looking for. The trick, and the point of this whole diatribe, is to help you show them that.

If you walk into an interview and try to pretend to be someone you're not, it's not going to work. It just won't. I've seen applicants walk into the room and try to be something they think I want to see, and it's like watching someone pound a square peg into a round hole.

Everything we've gone over up to this point is about effectively presenting what *you* personally have to offer. I'm not trying to make you into a Rick Hogan robotic interview clone. I'm simply giving you a framework to make sure you're showing your interviewers and evaluators the *best* side of yourself, not a completely different-than-normal side.

Most good interviewers can get a feel for whether an applicant is giving canned answers they think people want to hear, or whether they're being honest and sincere. Having seen both sides of that coin, honesty and sincerity always look better. Interviewers want to get to know the real you as much as they can in the limited time they have to meet with you. Give them the opportunity to do that by being yourself, not who you think they want you to be.

Part 7

Interview styles

Y ou've studied, and studied and studied some more. You've practiced your stories and worked on resolving conflicts. You bought a simulator program and flew it until your computer melted down. You are totally prepared in every possible way.

You walk into the interview, and instead of being friendly and welcoming, your interviewers' style is something you hadn't counted on. You get the feeling they're looking at you like a scientist studying an amoeba through a microscope, and there's a definite, "why should we hire you" vibe going on.

All of this catches you off guard and throws you off your game. You feel the pressure mounting and all of a sudden, things aren't going the way you want them to.

They ask you something simple like, "how many wings does the aircraft you're currently flying have?" and you just totally go blank.

The voice in your head is screaming, "YOU'RE SCREWING IT UP!"

And the next thing you know some jackass is writing a book about how you train-wrecked your interview.

An interviewer's style has a tremendous impact on the tone of your interview. We all want to walk into the interview room and be greeted by a warm and friendly face and have a pleasant, no stress experience, but it doesn't always work out that way. Your interviewers hold complete control over the tone of the interview by the method(s) they choose to employ.

If the tone is negative, which it can be, it's possible to get drawn into that negativity if you're not careful. If it's positive, which we all hope for, you can get *too* comfortable and subsequently start acting too casual. You have to be aware that there are as many different ways to interview as there are interviewers, and you may not necessarily enjoy the method chosen for you. Whatever tactic they employ, don't let it affect the presentation you are giving.

Most importantly, don't take the tone of your interview personally. If they find fault with something you've said or done, just take it with a smile, it's all part of the process.

The corporate world typically recognizes 4 fundamental interview styles: Relaxed, Intimidating, Friend, and Panel.

The "Relaxed" interview is typically designed to get better dialogue from the candidate by creating a comfortable and open atmosphere. "Intimidating" is just like it sounds. You turn up the pressure on a candidate and see how much they can take. A "Friend" based interview will have a candidate interviewed by someone who will be a co-worker as opposed to a supervisor. The logic here is that many applicants put on an interview face for supervisors but act differently around co-workers. A "Panel" interview consists of several members, each with different interview styles. This forces the candidate to react to different questions and different personalities.

As we all know, the aviation world is not quite the same as the corporate world. Aviation interviews will typically follow the fundamental baselines above, with some subtle differences.

Here are some examples of the core interview styles you can be faced with in a pilot interview, along with the best ways to deal with them:

The friendly interview

I would choose this type of interview over the alternatives any day, because it's the easiest to deal with. Everyone likes a friendly interview. They're comfortable and low stress, the interviewers are personable and easy to get along with. It's almost like sitting around talking with old friends.

Two weeks later, however, you get the "thanks, but no thanks" letter. It seemed like things went great. What happened?

Friendly interviews are sometimes almost enjoyable, but (and this is by design) they can be disarming. No matter how friendly your interview feels, you must remember that *you are in fact still being interviewed.* Don't lose focus on why you're there. You are still being evaluated even if it doesn't feel like it at the time.

You should walk a fine line in the friendly interview. You need to be personable, friendly, and conversational, but you can't relax to the point that you stop being professional. I've seen people get so relaxed in a friendly interview that they slouch way back in their chair, swing their arm over the top, and start joking and swearing like we're hanging out in a bar. You're not in a bar, however, and you're not hanging out with friends. You're being interviewed. Be friendly in kind, but never stop being professional.

The confrontational interview

This is the interview everyone dreads. You sit down and almost instantly feel like you're being disciplined for doing something wrong.

"Why did you make that decision?"

"Why did you record these times in your logbook this way?"

"There are a lot more qualified people out there, why should we hire you?"

There are no smiles and nothing to put you at ease in a confrontational interview. There are only hard questions, no positive feedback, and a general sense of disapproval. You just have to sit there with a smile on your face and answer each question in a friendly and professional manner. Here's the key to surviving the experience: *don't take any of it personally.* You're just experiencing a confrontational interview style. Your interviewers don't really dislike you, or think you're not qualified, or any other negative thing. If they did, they never would have brought you to the interview to begin with. They are trying to see how easily rattled you are.

I had a very confrontational interview several years ago.

"Those ACMI guys are pretty weird, aren't they? Does that mean you're weird?"

"Why would you go fly overseas? Couldn't you make it here?"

"Why are you using an electronic logbook? Where are your original endorsements? Are you trying to hide something? How do we know these times are accurate?"

The interview went on and on like this for the better part of an hour. The interviewer kept talking about how bad my previous companies were and wanted me to join in on putting them down. I just kept smiling and answering his questions in the most positive way possible, never saying anything negative about anyone. I left the interview knowing it had been designed to be confrontational, but still not caring for it (or the interviewer) very much.

After I was hired, I ran into that interviewer under different circumstances. He was a completely different person. He was friendly, personable, and actually acted like he was glad to see me on the property. The confrontational style is a tool he uses to try to learn about the applicants. It wouldn't be my choice, but it was his. It could be the choice of your interviewers' someday, and if it is, just don't get drawn into it. Stay friendly, happy, personable, and positive, no matter how negative or confrontational the line of questioning gets.

The stone-faced interview

This interviewer gives you absolutely no feedback to your answers, good or bad. It's like talking to a totem pole. You could jump up on the table and start doing the can-can, and your stone-faced interviewer would stare impassively and quietly wait for you to finish. The questions come out in a steady monotone. When you've finished your answer there is no reaction, just the next question.

I've had a couple of interviews like this as well, and honestly, I think this was harder to deal with than the confrontational one. At least if your interviewer is confrontational, you're getting *something* back, even if it's negative. Sometimes something is better than nothing. Sitting in the interview chair and trying to act friendly while your interviewer robotically works down a list of questions is tough. You have to handle the stone-faced interviewer just like you would a confrontational one. Don't let it affect you or change your demeanor. Maintain eye contact and stay friendly, upbeat, and positive.

Good cop, bad cop

This is a combination of the friendly and confrontational styles, and *almost always* happens in a panel interview. One or more interviewers will be very friendly, but there will be at least one who is confrontational or stone-faced. You will find yourself relating to the friendly members and excluding the odd one out, which is how you would react in a normal social situation. If you're talking to a group of people, and one is friendly while the other is clearly not, whom are you going to focus your conversation toward? Just like we talked about in the body language section, you need to continually divide your focus between everyone in the room. If you find yourself identifying more with one interviewer than the others, don't exclude the less friendly members of the group.

The tone can even change during the interview. It can go from friendly to confrontational and then back to friendly. Most interviews aren't completely one extreme or another, but fall somewhere in the middle. Recognize what is happening and why, and don't take anything personally. It's all strategies and gamesmanship. Regardless of the tone your interviewers are taking with you, don't allow it to affect your actions. Maintain your composure and continue to handle the questions the way you practiced.

Points to remember

✓ Your interview can be representative of any number of different tones or styles. Regardless of the style or tone your interviewers use, you must maintain your composure and produce your answers like you've practiced. Don't let them throw you off your game. Stay friendly and personable no matter how your interviewers may act towards you.

Part 8

Closing the interview

J ust like a flight isn't over until you run the shutdown checklist, your interview isn't over until you walk back through the front door. Finishing strong is equally important to starting strong.

A friend of mine who interviewed with United Airlines related this train wreck to me. Unfortunately, it was his.

United was his career goal for as long as I'd known him. When he got the interview, he was beyond excited. He studied for hours and hours on end. He bought simulator time, did the interview prep thing, the whole nine yards. If I had to put money on anyone being successful in an interview, it would have been him.

Interview day rolled around and he showed up in the expensive, tailored suit he'd bought just for the occasion. Every part of the screening process leading up to the interview went great. He was invited back for the interview and the captain and HR representatives introduced themselves. It was semi-confrontational, which was par for the course for United back in the late '90s, but nothing he wasn't expecting and ready for. Things progressed along and it's all going fairly by the numbers.

Finally, the interview was wrapping up, and the captain stood and shook his hand, saying, "I have just one last question for you. What are our names?"

They'd introduced themselves to my friend less than an hour ago, but he was so focused on the interview he hadn't really even heard them. During the introduction he said hello, shook their hands, and then went right into interview mode.

"I'm sorry, I can't remember," he admitted.

"OK. Thanks for coming in," the captain replied.

He didn't get the job. It was a tough blow, and he attributes it to not paying enough attention to the names of his interviewers.

You can't ever know exactly what happened in an interview if you weren't there. When people relate their interview stories, they tend to remember the good points while leaving out the bad. I can tell you, unequivocally, not remembering the names of your interviewers will not help you in any way.

The hiring process in the airline world is a marathon, not a sprint. You may have already noticed that. Don't blow all your preparation and a potentially great interview by tripping over your shoelaces right in front of the finish line.

Closing the interview is an equally important part of the whole process. When you meet someone for the first time, at the end of your meeting do you just stand up, turn around, and walk out of the room without saying another word? If you do, I'd like to recommend another book called *How to NOT be a Social Idiot.*

When you conclude a meeting with someone, especially in an interview setting, thank everyone for their time. At the very least, thank them for giving you the opportunity to meet with them. Have a plan in place for what you want to say (again, don't have a script, but have an outline of how you want to close). Shake hands with everyone when you leave. Completing the interview at long last is a huge relief; just don't mentally check out too early at the expense of some common courtesy.

1. The same rules for handshakes apply. While I'd like to make this book as long and boring and repetitive as possible, I'll simply refer you back to that section.

2. It's nice to use the names of your interviewers in closing. It shows you've taken an interest in them as they have in you for the last hour. Say, as you're shaking hands, "Captain Courageous, thank you for giving me the opportunity to come in and meet with you. Ms. Ratchett, thank you for your time."

3. I am personally terrible with names, so I use a memory aid. I come up with a rhyme or some type of association to jog my memory. Leslie has long hair. Captain Johnson is John's son. If you're good with names, don't change what works. If you have the short-term memory of a gnat (like myself), come up with a way to remember the people you're meeting for the next hour.

4. Don't address your interviewers by their first name in a professional setting.

5. Use appropriate titles. These should become apparent when you're introduced at the beginning of the interview. If a man or woman introduces himself or herself as Captain So-and-so, use that title when you address them. If they simply introduce themselves as Travis Bickle and Marie Antoinette, use Mr. Bickle and Ms. Antoinette. Ms. (pronounced Miz) is the title used before

a woman's surname when her marital status is either unknown or irrelevant.

One common question I've asked and *been* asked in every single interview I've ever been involved with in the history of the world: "Do you have any questions for us?"

Interviewers spend all day coming up with subtle, tricky questions designed to pry every bit of useful information out of you. They like to answer questions once in a while, provided they're not too hard or beyond the limited scope of what they know for interview purposes. *Asking* questions is a good indication of someone who is personable, actively participating in the whole process, and generally excited about the prospective job.

This is also a good place to incorporate some company specific knowledge as well:

"What do you think of the new 787s the company has on order?"

"How is the new expansion into Asia going?"

"How long do you think hiring will be going on?"

Try to come up with something relevant, and something your interviewers will enjoy answering. Don't ask about something too controversial. For example, if the company and the pilots are renegotiating a contract, that's a good subject to stay away from. I would stay away from any subject that has the potential to polarize someone one way or another.

Here's an example of how a well-placed and well-timed question can work to your benefit:

I interviewed with the Chief Pilot of a regional airline right when the EMB-145s were first being produced. This particular company had placed a huge order for them. During the course of the interview, I heard the Chief Pilot mention how he was part of the implementation team for this aircraft. I knew a little (very little) about the aircraft from an article I'd read a few days before the interview. I knew about the order from researching the company, and I thought the article might come in handy.

When the interview started wrapping up, I got the standard, "Do you have any questions for me?"

"I heard you mention you were working on the EMB-145 project. That seems like a really great airplane. What do you think of it?"

You should have seen his face light up. The interview went on for another 20 minutes, only it wasn't an interview at that point. It was the chief pilot talking about how much he liked the EMB-145. All I did was sit back and go along for the ride.

I got a personal call with a job offer the next day. Everyone else waited over a week for a letter in the mail.

Closing the interview well is as important as starting the interview well. Don't let out your sigh of relief and go back to being the normal, every-day slob you usually are until you walk back through your door at home.

Points to remember

- ✓ Always close your interview with a handshake and a word of thanks.
- ✓ Remember your interviewers' names, and address them with appropriate titles when you thank them.
- ✓ Try to have at least one good question for your interviewers when they conclude the interview.

Don't be picky about starting class

I worked with a pilot who was getting furloughed from a Legacy Carrier, and we got him into the hiring pool at one of the top ACMI carriers in the industry. This company operated both 747 Classics and 747-400s.

He called me a couple of weeks after receiving notification that he was in the pool and said, "Hey, they offered me a class date but I turned it down."

My brain didn't process that fully for a second, and I responded, "Hey that's grea...wait...what?"

"Yeah, they said the class was for the classic, and I told them I wanted to wait for the 400. They weren't sure when they were going to have a 400 class, they said maybe in a few weeks."

"Okay," I replied, "but aren't you getting furloughed soon? I thought starting class sooner would have been better than later?"

"I can wait a couple of extra weeks. I'd rather have the 400 type anyway."

So he waited. And waited. And waited. After about four weeks of not hearing anything, he called me and asked what he should do. I said it couldn't hurt to get in touch with his point-of-contact and inquire about his status, so he called them up.

Long story short: the HR representative said that since he wasn't interested in flying the classic for their company, he'd been placed at the bottom of the pool. The very bottom. Even below the people who had yet to interview. This was her way of saying if the classic wasn't good enough, they probably didn't need him. He never ended up getting another class date offer.

There are a million different reasons you may not be able to make the first class they offer you. Just keep in mind there are never any guarantees of future classes. Also keep in mind that the people who *are* starting class ahead of you will have first choice of schedule, vacation, bases, equipment, and upgrade, etc.

I got hired once at the very beginning of a wave that was supposed to total up to three hundred new hires. They stopped running classes after hiring fifty (of which I was about number forty eight). The only class you can guarantee getting into is the one they are offering you right now. The sooner you can actually get into new-hire training and get a seniority number, the better.

If you really, really can't make the one they are offering you, be reasonable in your explanation. Just like we talked about in using good judgment when choosing past experiences to relate, use good judgment if you're deferring a class. Don't tell them it's because you don't want a particular base/equipment combination, because part of accepting employment with any company is accepting what that company has to offer. And guess what? Most companies are proud of the fleets and base structures they've built. If you act like you're too good for some of the aircraft they're operating, they may agree with you.

Sometimes, it just doesn't work out

You got the gouge, rented a sim, bought a new suit, and practiced your answers until you could say them backwards in pig Latin if you wanted to. The interview seemed like it went fine. You even effectively dodged your logbook when your confrontational interviewer threw it at you. All that, and you still got a letter that says, "Thanks for coming in, but..."

Sometimes, it's just not meant to be. Don't let a disappointment, no matter how bitter it may be, discourage you from trying to reach your career goals. Use the experience you've gained to be successful in your next interview, instead of letting it prevent you from moving forward.

People can handle an interview rejection in one of two ways:

1. They throw their hands up, accept defeat, and end up stuck in the job they wanted to move on from, growing bitter and resentful of their lot in life over time. They will eventually end up living in a dark cave where they compulsively caress a ring, muttering, "My precious..." over and over again.

2. They use the rejection as a constructive experience. They continue their efforts, and even re-apply to the company that rejected them once they fall within the re-application window. The will end up reaching their goals, even if they're not the specific goals they initially expected.

I know a lot of people, both inside and outside of aviation, who have gotten their dream job on the second interview. I know even more people who ended up with a "dream" job they weren't even aware they wanted to begin with. Industry forces pushed them away from the career path they envisioned, but they forged ahead and made a new path that wasn't necessarily the one they expected. Sometimes it's the unexpected journeys in life that end up being the most fun.

One of the most important components to succeeding is being tenacious in your pursuit of it. Don't let a bump in the road prevent you from achieving what you set out to do. I know getting rejected hurts, whether it's asking a girl to prom or interviewing for a job you've wanted your whole life, but you have to push through that hurt and use it to channel your efforts. Sometimes, you need to face adversity to be successful.

Points to remember

- ✓ Take the first class you're offered, if you can.
- ✓ Sometimes, no matter how hard you try, it just doesn't happen. Don't let rejection prevent you from reaching your goals.

Part 9

Visualize who you need to be

Imagine you're going on a flight, along with your entire family and all your friends. Everyone who means anything to you in the world is going to be on this airplane. It's going to be a long flight, and you're told right up front there will be an emergency the pilots will have to deal with (but hey, the flight's free!).

The emergency might be small, or it might be huge. All the engines could fail, or there could be hijackers on board (that would actually be *your* fault, since they're all your friends and family), or one of the flight attendants could fall down and break his/her leg. All you know for sure is that there will be an emergency, without a doubt, and the flight crew will have to handle it.

In exchange for your taking this flight with the unknown emergency, you get to walk into a roomful of pilots and pick who will be flying the airplane. You've got all day to choose.

What type of pilot are you looking for? Probably someone capable of dealing with anything safely, efficiently, and effectively. The pilot you are looking for is the same one your interviewers are looking for.

One guy doesn't have a suit on and looks like he just rolled out of bed. Will he do the best job? Here's a lady with spelling errors all over her application and who hands you a logbook that looks like it's been submerged in water. Do you want her at the controls? Here's some guy who can't look you in the eyes and talks to his hands. Will he be a good choice? I know I probably wouldn't want to be on these pilots' aircraft on a good day, let alone when they had an emergency to deal with.

Now wait. Here's someone who's dressed very professionally, present themselves well, and communicate effectively. Their paperwork is perfect. Would this person be a good candidate? Possibly, but you need more information. Give them a written test to find out what they know. Stick them in a simulator and see if they can fly. Now you can personally ask them some questions. Go over some technical items to see if they know what they're talking about. Talk about some situations that don't necessarily have right or wrong answers. Maybe this line of questioning will give you some insight into what makes them tick and how they solve problems.

Put all the information you've collected together, and then ask yourself if this is the person you want in control of your flight. The lives of you, your family, and your friends depend on your decision. Who would you pick?

You're asking the same questions your interviewers are asking themselves, and you're both looking for the same thing. You are both looking for a person who's competent, personable, capable, and up to any task.

This is the person *you* need to be. And it's the person you can be, if you prepare the right way. As I said before, this isn't *The Quick and Easy Guide to Scam your Interviewers and Fool Them into Hiring You*. This is a system which, if you follow it, will show your interviewers what they *need* to see in order to put you in the cockpit of an aircraft that their future, financially and otherwise, depends on. You are the person they want, just give them what they need, and you'll be boring holes through the sky for fun and profit in no time.

Conclusion

You've reached the end. Congratulations!

You may be saying to yourself, "I hope this guy knows what he's talking about."

You've got a lot riding on it, I know. I can give you the assurance that it does work. I've used it, my friends and clients have used it, and it works. The thing to remember is that you get out of it what you put into it.

Anything worth doing in life takes effort. Taking all the guesswork out of an interview takes *a lot* of time and effort. But it is time and effort well spent.

The career train doesn't come around too often. When it hits your stop, you'd better be ready to jump on or you risk getting stuck somewhere you hadn't planned.

Walk into your interview and honestly say to yourself, "I've done everything humanly possible to get ready for this."

The rest is in the hands of the interview gods.

I'm confident if you use the methods I've outlined here you will be successful. The downside is you probably won't have an exciting story, because good interviews fade from memory fairly quickly. If you want to tell me how things worked out, or how they didn't, or just tell me you think I'm full of it, send an email to rick@airline-career.net. I'd love to hear your story: good, bad, or indifferent. I promise you won't become the next Interview Train Wreck subject. Maybe ;-)

Appendix: Interview Question Study Guide

S o I harped and harped about how you need to find your own answers to questions. That is a true statement. You still need to go through the gouge for whatever company you interview with and find out what they focus on. This is a reference guide to what I consider the foundation of what most airline interviews are built upon. This is the meat and potatoes. You won't be asked everything listed here, and you may be asked something that isn't, but this is a good starting point. This is the stuff you need to know for any interview because it's fundamental. If you walk into an interview and don't have a good working knowledge of the items that follow, you may as well just leave your pants at home.

If you can't remember the molecular formula for type II de-icing fluid, that probably won't be a big deal. If you blank out on one of the review items I've included here, it may raise a red flag with your interviewer.

I've chosen the subjective question examples from gouge I've carefully gone through for almost every airline interview out there. The questions I've included are, again, the core fundamental questions you can be asked. You won't get all the questions here, but I guarantee you'll get some. If it's not the exact question, it will be something similar. Have solid, well flowing answers to everything I've listed, and you'll be ready for whatever they throw at you.

As always, if you think something is missing, you think it's great, or you think this guide should be used for bathroom tissue, email me at rick@airline-career.net.

Technical Review

Regulations

What is the FAA alcohol limit?

- Can't use alcohol while on duty
- Can't be under the influence of alcohol while on duty
- Maximum blood alcohol level is 0.04
- No alcohol within 8 hours of duty

(91.17)

IFR Fuel requirements

- Domestic
    - Complete flight to destination
    - Fly from destination to alternate airport (most distant alternate if more than one)
    - Fly for 45 minutes at normal cruise speed
- Flag Operations
    - Fly to and land at destination
    - 10 percent of the total time required to fly from departure to, and land at, destination
    - Fly to and land at the most distant alternate airport
    - 30 minutes at holding speed at 1,500 ft above the alternate airport (or the destination airport if no alternate is required)
    - (Island Reserve only) To fly to destination and thereafter to fly for at least two hours at normal cruising fuel consumption

(91.167, 121.639, 121.645)

Airspeed Limits

- 10,000 ft or above: no limit
- Under 10,000 ft: 250 knots
    - It's a subtle distinction, but *at* 10,000 ft there is no speed limit
- Under Class B or in a VFR corridor: 200 knots
- Within 4 NM of Class C or D and at or below 2500 ft AGL: 200 knots

(91.117)

When is RVR controlling?

Where RVR is reported, it is controlling for takeoff and landing.

(121.655)

What is controlling if RVR is not reported?

The ceiling and visibility values in the main body of the latest weather report control takeoffs, landings and instrument approach procedures. However, if the latest weather report, including an oral report from the control tower, contains a visibility value specified as runway visibility or runway visual range for a particular runway of an airport, that specified value controls.

(121.655)

When do you need a takeoff alternate (Part 121)?

When weather conditions at the takeoff airport are below the certificate holder's landing minimums. A takeoff alternate is prudent if the weather is below the certificate holder's single engine landing minimums.

(121.617)

How far away can a takeoff alternate be from the departure airport?

- Two engine aircraft: one hour, normal cruise speed, one engine inoperative
- Three or more engine aircraft: two hours, normal cruise speed, one engine inoperative

(121.617)

Destination alternate requirements, Part 91 and 121

- Part 91
    - +/-1 hour, weather is at least 2000 ft ceiling and 3 SM visibility
- Part 121
    - same as part 91, but you need a second alternate if the weather at destination and the first alternate are marginal

(91.167, 121.619)

What is the minimum weather required to list an airport as an alternate?

- Part 91
    - Precision approach: 600 ft ceiling and 2 SM visibility
    - Non-precision approach: 800 ft ceiling and 2 SM visibility
- Part 121
    - Weather must be above the minimums listed in the airline's operation specifications for that airport

(91.169, 121.625)

What are standard takeoff weather minimums?

- Aircraft with 2 engines or less: 1 SM
- Aircraft with more than 2 engines: ½ SM

(91.175, 121.651)

If the visibility is reported below the published minimums, can you start the approach?

No. Under part 121, the visibility must be greater than or equal to the published minima to initiate the approach.

(121.651)

If the ceiling is reported below approach minimums, can you start the approach?

Yes. Under part 121, the *visibility* must be greater than or equal to the published minima to initiate the approach.

(121.651)

If you are inside the final approach fix, can you continue the approach if the reported visibility goes below the published minimums?

Yes. Under part 121, if you are established on the final approach segment the flight visibility is controlling.

(121.651)

Where is the final approach fix on an ILS?

Glideslope intercept at the published intercept altitude, or glideslope intercept at a lower altitude if assigned by ATC.

(Pilot/Controller Glossary)

When can you descend below DH/MDA

- Flight visibility is not less than the visibility required for the approach
- Aircraft can land in the touchdown zone using normal descent rates and normal maneuvers
- You can descend to 100 ft above the touchdown zone elevation with only the approach lights in sight
- You can land if you see:
  - Red side row bars
  - Red terminating bars
  - Threshold, threshold markings, threshold lights
  - Touchdown zone, touchdown zone markings, touchdown zone lights
  - Runway, runway markings, runway lights
  - Runway end identifier lights (REIL)
  - Visual approach slope indicator (VASI)

(121.651)

What is the minimum obstacle clearance required in mountainous terrain?

Two thousand feet above highest obstacle within 4 NM, of course.
(91.177)

What is the minimum obstacle clearance required in non-mountainous terrain?

One thousand feet above highest obstacle within 4 NM, of course.
(91.177)

What are lost communication procedures?

- If VMC is encountered after communication is lost, stay in VMC and land as soon as practicable
- Route, in order of ATC preference:
  - Route assigned by ATC in last clearance
  - If being radar vectored, the direct route from the point of failure to the fix, route or airway specified in the vectoring clearance
  - In absence of an assigned route, the route ATC advised you to expect in a future clearance
  - In the absence of an assigned or expected route, the route filed in your flight plan
- Altitude, highest of:
  - Last assigned altitude
  - Minimum altitude for IFR flight operations (MEA)
  - Altitude advised to expect

- Leave Clearance Limit:
  - If the clearance limit is a fix from which an approach begins, start descent as close to EFC as possible. If no EFC, start descent at ETA as figured from filed time en route.
  - If the clearance limit is not a fix from which an approach begins, leave the fix at your EFC (if received) or arrival over the fix, then continue to a fix from which an approach begins. Start descent and approach to arrive at ETA.
  - If the clearance limit is a fix from which an approach begins, proceed to the fix that begins the approach and start decent and approach at EFC (if received), or ETA.

(91.185)

What is "sterile cockpit"?

Sterile cockpit refers to the critical phase of flight, which includes taxi, takeoff and landing, and all other flight operations conducted below 10,000 ft, except cruise flight. During sterile cockpit, no pilot may perform any duties except those required for the safe operation of the aircraft.
(121.542)

When is DME required?

DME is required if you are flying at or above FL240 and using VORs for navigation.
(91.205)

What is a Minimum Equipment List (MEL)?

The MEL establishes which systems or components may be inoperative and the airplane still flown legally. With systems inoperative, the airplane must be operated in accordance with the limitations specified in the MEL.
(91.213)

Your aircraft has an inoperative system that is not referenced in the MEL. Can you depart?

No.

(91.213)

Aeronautical Information Manual

Describe runway centerline lights
- Runway centerline lights are spaced at 50 ft intervals
- White lights until last 3,000 ft
- Alternating white and red 3,000 ft-1,000 ft
- Red last 1,000 ft

(AIM 2-1-5)

Describe runway edge lights?
White, except on instrument runways; yellow replaces white on the last 2,000 ft or half the runway length, whichever is less.

(AIM 2-1-4)

What color are taxiway lead off lights?
Alternate green and yellow lights, beginning with green.

(AIM 2-1-5)

What color are taxiway edge lights?
Blue.

(AIM 2-1-9)

What color are taxiway centerline lights?
Green.

(AIM 2-1-9)

How far out can a VASI be seen?
VASI lights are visible from 3-5 miles during the day and up to 20 miles or more at night.

(AIM 2-1-2)

Does a VASI provide obstruction clearance?

The visual glide path of the VASI provides obstruction clearance 10 degrees either side of centerline up to 4 NM from the runway threshold. (AIM 2-1-2)

What is the advantage of a three bar VASI?

A normal glide angle is afforded both high and low cockpit aircraft. (AIM 2-1-2)

What would a three bar VASI look like if on the lower glide path?

Two red bars over one white bar. (AIM 2-1-2)

Do you have to fly the VASI glide slope?

Yes. In class B, C, or D airspace if the runway has a VASI you must fly at or above the slope. (91.129, 91.130, 91.131)

At what increments are the touchdown zone markings?

Every 500 ft. (AIM 2-3-3)

How far down the runway do the touchdown zone markings extend?

Three thousand feet, or to within 900 ft of the midpoint if touchdown zone markers extend from the other end of the runway. (AIM 2-3-3)

What is an ILS critical area?

An area near the localizer or glide slope antenna where potential disturbances to an ILS localizer and glide slope may occur when surface vehicles or aircraft are operated.

(AIM 2-3-5)

When do you have to hold short of the ILS critical area?

When instructed by ATC to "Hold short of runway xx approach area."

(AIM 2-3-5)

Under what weather conditions will the ILS critical area be protected?

Eight hundred foot ceiling and/or 2 miles visibility.

(AIM 1-1-11)

What altitudes does RVSM airspace include?

FL290 - FL410 (inclusive).

(AIM 4-6-1)

What does RVSM provide?

A one thousand foot vertical separation from opposite direction aircraft.

(AIM 4-6-2)

What equipment is required for flight in RVSM airspace?

- The aircraft must be equipped with two operational independent altitude measurement systems
- The aircraft must be equipped with at least one automatic altitude control system
- The aircraft must be equipped with an altitude alert system that signals an alert when the altitude displayed to the flight crew deviates from the selected altitude

(FAR Part 91 appendix G)

When are wingtip vortices the most dangerous?

When an airplane is heavy, clean (gear and flaps up), and slow.

(AIM 7-3-3)

What is the most dangerous wind condition for wake turbulence?

A light quartering tailwind. The upwind vortex will remain on the runway longer and the tailwind will cause the wake turbulence to drift farther down the runway.

(AIM 7-3-4)

When landing behind a heavy aircraft, what is the preferred flight path and touchdown point?

- Fly a higher path and upwind, if possible
- Touchdown after the heavy aircraft's touchdown point

(AIM 7-3-6)

When landing on a runway where a heavy aircraft just departed, what is the preferred touchdown point?

Land prior to the heavy aircraft's rotation point.

(AIM 7-3-6)

When taking off behind a heavy aircraft, what is the preferred rotation point and climb out path?

- Rotate prior to the heavy aircraft's rotation point
- Climb on a higher path and upwind, if possible

(AIM 7-3-6)

When taking off from a runway where a heavy aircraft just landed, what is the preferred rotation point?

Rotate beyond the heavy aircraft's touchdown point.

(AIM 7-3-6)

How are aircraft classes defined for wake turbulence separation?

- Heavy- Aircraft capable of takeoff weights of more than 255,000 pounds, whether or not they are operating at this weight during a particular phase of flight.
- Large- Aircraft of more than 41,000 pounds, maximum certificated takeoff weight, up to 255,000 pounds
- Small- Aircraft of 41,000 pounds or less maximum certificated takeoff weight

(Pilot/Controller Glossary)

Wake turbulence separation

En route separation (aircraft behind is at the same altitude or less than 1000 ft below)

Heavy	Behind	Heavy	4 miles
Large/Heavy	Behind	B757	4 miles
Small	Behind	B757	5 miles
Small/Large	Behind	Heavy	5 miles

Landing separation provided to small aircraft (aircraft ahead is over the landing threshold)

Small	Behind	Heavy	6 miles
Small	Behind	B757	5 miles
Small	Behind	Large	4 miles

Takeoff separation (same runway, crossing runway, or close parallel runway)

- Two minutes or the appropriate 4/5 miles separation behind a heavy/B575

(AIM 7-3-9)

What is a NOTAM?

NOTAMS contain time critical information that is either temporary or there is not enough time to put the information into a publication or chart. (AIM 5-1-3)

What are the categories of NOTAMs?

- NOTAM (D) = distant, large no go issues. Examples: airport closure, runway closure. All ATC facilities have access to these NOTAMs.
- NOTAM (L) = local, smaller items. Examples: taxiway closures and airport lighting that do not affect instrument procedures.
- NOTAM (FDC) = Flight Data Center, regulatory. Examples: change of MEA en-route, change to an instrument approach procedure. FSSs maintain a list of these within 400 miles of their facility.

(AIM 5-1-3)

What action should a pilot take if within 3 minutes of a clearance limit, and further clearance has not been received?

Start speed reduction to cross the fix at or below the maximum holding speed. Prior to the fix, ask ATC for holding instructions. If unable to get instructions prior to the fix, enter a standard hold on the current course and get further instructions. (AIM 5-3-7)

What are the Maximum Holding Airspeeds?

- 0 - 6,000 ft MSL   200 KIAS
- 6,001 ft – 14,000 ft MSL   230 KIAS
- 14,001 ft MSL and above   265 KIAS

(AIM 5-3-7)

When is a pilot expected to slow to holding speed?

When aircraft is 3 minutes or less from the holding fix. (AIM 5-3-7)

What is a standard holding pattern?

- Right turns
- Inbound leg 1 minute at or below 14,000 ft MSL
- Inbound leg 1½ minutes above 14,000 ft MSL

(AIM 5-3-7)

What is the width of an airway or route?

Four NM on each side of centerline.

(AIM 5-3-5)

What are the VOR service volumes?

Terminal	1000 to 12,000 AGL		25 NM
Low	1000 to 18,000 AGL		40 NM
High	1000 to 14,500 AGL		40 NM
	14,500 to 18,000 AGL	100 NM	
	18,000 to 45,000 AGL	130 NM	
	45,000 to 60,000 AGL	100 NM	

(AIM 1-1-8)

When is RVR reported?

When the prevailing visibility is 1 mile or less and/or the RVR is 6,000 ft or less.

(AIM 7-1-15)

When is a procedure turn not required?

- "NoPT" or "No Procedure Turn" noted on chart
- Holding in lieu of procedure turn
- Conducting a timed approach from a holding fix
- Radar vectors to final

(AIM 5-4-9)

When is a procedure turn or hold in lieu of PT required?

When depicted on the approach chart.

(AIM 5-4-9)

Where is the missed approach point on an ILS?

Arrival at decision altitude/height on glide slope.

(Pilot/Controller Glossary)

Aerodynamics/Performance

Define V1.

Takeoff decision speed; if you lose an engine on the takeoff roll prior to V1, you can abort and stop on the remaining runway (accelerate-stop distance). If you lose an engine after V1, you are not guaranteed to be able to stop on the runway but are able to take off and climb to 35 ft by the end of the runway (accelerate-go distance). Lose engine prior to V1=stop; after V1=go.

Define Vr.

Rotation speed.

Define V2.

Takeoff safety speed; the speed to maintain required climb gradient if you lose an engine at V1.

Define Vx

Best angle of climb speed with all engines operating.

Define Vy

Best rate of climb speed with all engines operating.

Define Va

Design maneuvering speed; the maximum speed at which abrupt, full deflection, control input will not cause the aircraft to exceed its structural limit. At Va, the aircraft will stall prior to structural damage occurring.

Define Vmu

Minimum unstick speed; lowest possible speed at which the airplane will lift off the ground.

Define Vs

The   stalling   speed   in   the   clean   (cruise)   configuration.

Define Vso

The stalling speed in the landing configuration.

Define Vs1, Vs2, etc.

The stalling speed in a specific configuration, as defined in the aircraft pilot operating handbook.

What do you do with an engine failure after V1, but prior to V2?

Continue takeoff.

On a long runway and you lose an engine after V1, what do you do?

Continue takeoff.

What is a balanced field?

The accelerate stop distance (accelerate to V1, lose an engine, stop on the runway) equals the accelerate go distance (accelerate to V1, lose an engine, continue takeoff and climb to 35 ft).

Why is there a longer takeoff roll with a tailwind?

The speed required for takeoff is a function of the speed of the air over the wing required to generate sufficient lift. For example: If 120 knots of airspeed over the wing is required and there is a 10-knot tailwind, then the airplane must accelerate to 130 knots prior to getting the required lift.

Takeoff distance, groundspeed, indicated airspeed difference when hot vs. cold.

Indicated airspeed doesn't change because it represents the speed of the air over the wing accurately regardless of temperature. Hot air is less dense than cold air; therefore, groundspeed will increase for a given indicated airspeed. Because of the increased groundspeed, the takeoff distance will also increase.

Takeoff distance, groundspeed, indicated airspeed difference when high altitude vs. low altitude airport.

Indicated airspeed doesn't change because it represents the speed of the air over the wing accurately regardless of altitude. The air at a high altitude airport is less dense than a lower altitude airport; therefore, groundspeed will increase for a given indicated airspeed. Because of the increased groundspeed, the takeoff distance will also increase.

What factors influence takeoff distance?

Weight, altitude, temperature, wind, configuration (flap setting), runway slope, runway condition (slush, standing water).

What are the types of hydroplaning?

- Dynamic- occurs at high speed as the tire rides on a layer of water. The approximate speed that dynamic hydroplaning occurs is the square root of the tire pressure times nine.
- Reverted Rubber- occurs when a tire skids on a smooth wet or icy surface and generates heat. That heat causes the water under the tire to steam, which lifts the tire off the surface. The heat also changes (reverts) the thin outermost layer of the tire into a gummy substance, further reducing friction. This can occur at any speed above 20 knots.
- Viscous- occurs when the tires lose traction when going over already low friction surfaces, like painted or rubber coated portions of taxiways and runways, where the friction is further reduced because of water. It is the most common type of hydroplaning and can occur at very low speeds.

What are the different altitudes?

- Absolute: above terrain
- Pressure: above standard datum plate
- Density: pressure altitude corrected for temperature
- True: above mean sea level

What are the different airspeeds?

- Indicated: as displayed
- Calibrated: indicated corrected for installation error
- Equivalent: calibrated for compressibility effect
- True: equivalent corrected for air density
- Ground: true corrected for wind

What is Mach number?

The speed of an aircraft divided by the speed of sound. Mach .80 means the aircraft is traveling at 80% the speed of sound.

How does moving CG forward affect performance?

It decreases performance because of the increased tail down force required, generating more drag.

Climb relationship of airspeeds?

Climb at constant IAS, increased TAS

Climb at constant Mach, decreased TAS

Advantage of swept wing aircraft?

Delays the onset of Mach buffet allowing for faster cruise speeds.

Disadvantage of swept wing aircraft?

- Wing tip stalls first
- Increased takeoff speed
- Increased stall speed

What is Dutch roll?

Dutch roll is an aggravated flying state where a yawing moment will cause the forward moving wing to generate lift raising that wing, but also increasing drag on that side, thereby causing an opposite and increased yawing motion. The opposite wing then raises and creates yaw. The cycle will continue and worsen if not stopped. It is more prevalent in swept wings, at altitude where the air density makes the rudder less effective.

What do modern airplanes have to counter Dutch Roll?

A yaw damper, which makes quick small adjustments to the rudder to eliminate Dutch roll before it becomes a problem.

What is coffin corner?

When stall buffet speed increases with altitude as the air becomes less dense. Mach buffet speed decreases with altitude because air temperature decreases with altitude. Coffin corner occurs when an airplane climbs so high that the margin between stall buffet and Mach buffet approaches zero. Slowing down would cause the aircraft to enter a stall buffet while speeding up would cause it to enter the Mach buffet.

How do you exit coffin corner?

Maintain airspeed and start a slow descent to increase the margin between the buffets.

What is critical Mach?

Critical Mach is the airspeed at which air moving over the wing reaches Mach 1.0. Because air over the wing is accelerated, this will occur when the airplane is flying slower than Mach 1.0.

What is Mach tuck?

When a shock wave forms, the air behind it has increased static pressure and reduced energy. When the airplane goes faster than critical Mach, a shock wave forms and the boundary layer behind the shock wave may separate from the wing. On a swept wing aircraft this happens at the wing root first, causing the center of pressure of the wing to move aft, causing a diving moment.

What is Mach buffet?

When the airplane goes faster than critical Mach, a shock wave forms, and the boundary layer behind the shock wave may separate from the wing. The separating air is turbulent, causing fluttering of the control surfaces resulting in a buffet similar in feel to a stall buffet.

What are the effects of an aft CG?

- Stall speed decreases
- Cruise speed increases
- Maneuverability increases
- Stability decreases
- Aircraft range increases

What are vortex generators and where would you find them on a wing?

They increase the energy in the boundary layer to delay the separation of airflow and increase control effectiveness. Vortex generators are small tabs mounted perpendicular to the top of the airfoil. They act exactly like wings and produce vortices, which add energetic, fast airflow into the boundary layer.

The pitot tube is blocked, what would your indications be?

Your airspeed indicator will act like an altimeter. As you climb, the airspeed will increase, and decrease as you descend.

Static port is blocked. What would your indications be?

The altimeter will stop at the altitude when the blockage occurs. Airspeed will show artificially low if above the blockage altitude, and artificially high below the blocked altitude.

Effects of winglets?

Winglets interrupt wingtip vortices and reduce induced drag.

Explain the difference between induced and parasite drag.

Induced drag is caused by the development of lift. It is most prevalent at low airspeeds. Parasite drag is all drag not caused by the development of lift. The two most common types of parasite drag are skin friction drag and form drag.

What is L/D max?

- The airspeed at which the difference between lift and drag is the greatest
- Jet aircraft: Maximum endurance airspeed, max engine out glide
- Prop aircraft: Maximum range, max engine out glide

Why does stall speed increase with altitude?

Increase in altitude decreases density and increases the true airspeed at which a stall will occur.

Describe ground effect.

When an airplane is near the ground, the wing tip vortices are decreased, thereby decreasing the induced drag produced by the wing.

What is the definition of critical engine?

The engine whose failure results in the most adverse effects on the aircraft's handling and performance.

What is adverse yaw?

Yaw produced in the opposite direction of a banked turn requiring rudder input to counter. As an example, in a left turn the right wing is raised using extra lift. Extra lift also creates extra drag on the right wing, which pulls the nose to the right. Left rudder is required to counter this moment and coordinate the turn.

What is longitudinal stability?

Stability of the airplane along its longitudinal axis (nose to tail) and about its lateral axis (wing tip to wing tip). In simple terms, it is nose up/down stability.

What is static stability?

Static stability is the initial tendency of an object to return to equilibrium. Positive static stability means the object will attempt to return to equilibrium. Negative static stability means the object will continue to diverge away from equilibrium once disturbed. Neutral static stability means the object has neither tendency. As an example, if the yoke of an airplane is straight and level flight is moved aft then released and the airplane has positive stability the nose will fall once released; if negative stability, the nose will continue to rise once released, and if neutral stability, the nose stays in the position where the yoke was released.

What is the region of reverse command?

At airspeeds below L/Dmax, total drag increases as the airspeed decreases due to an increase in induced drag. The slower the airspeed below L/Dmax, the more power is required.

Weather

How long is a METAR valid?

It is a report, valid only when it is issued.

Decode METAR

```
METAR   KRJH   231955Z   AUTO   32012G17KT   280V350   2SM
R27/P6000FT  -RA BR
BKN015  OVC025  09/05  A2990  RMK  A02  PK  WND  31020/28
WSHFT   1920   VIS   3/4V1   1/2   VIS   3/4   RWY27   RAB24
CIG013V017  CIG  017  RWY27  PRESFR  SLP125  P0004  60010
T00940046 10099 21014 58033 TSNO $
```

METAR

TYPE OF REPORT

METAR: hourly (scheduled) report; SPECI: special (unscheduled) report.

KRJH

ICAO STATION (location) IDENTIFIER

Four character ICAO location identifier.

231955Z

DATE/TIME group

All dates and times in UTC using a 24-hour clock; two-digit date and four-digit time; always appended with Z to indicate UTC.

AUTO

REPORT MODIFIER

AUTO: Indicates a fully automated report with no human intervention. It is removed when an observer logs onto the system. COR: Indicates a corrected observation. No modifier indicates human observer or automated system with human logged on for oversight functions.

32012G17KT 280V350
WIND DIRECTION AND SPEED
Direction in tens of degrees from true north (first three digits); next two digits: speed in whole knots; if needed, include character as: Gusts (character) followed by maximum observed speed; always appended with KT to indicate knots; 00000KT for calm; if direction varies by 60 degrees or more and speed greater than 6 knots, a variable wind direction group is reported, otherwise omitted. If wind direction is variable and speed 6 knots or less, replace wind direction with VRB followed by wind speed in knots.

2SM
PREVAILING VISIBLITY
Prevailing visibility in statute miles and fractions with space between whole miles and fractions; always appended with SM VISIBILITY to indicate statute miles; values <1/4SM reported as M1/4SM.

R27/P6000FT
RUNWAY VISUAL RANGE
A 10-minute RVR evaluation value in hundreds of feet is reported if prevailing visibility is < or = 1 mile or RVR < or = 6000 feet; always appended with FT to indicate feet; value prefixed with M or P to indicate value is lower or higher than the reportable RVR value.

-RA BR

WEATHER PHENOMENA

Qualifier of Intensity or Proximity

-      Light

(no sign)   Moderate

+   Heavy

VC   Vicinity (5-10SM) but not at aerodrome

Descriptor

MI   Shallow

BL   Blowing

BC   Patches

SH   Showers

PR   Partial

DR   Drifting

TS   Thunderstorm

FZ   Freezing

Precipitation

DZ   Drizzle

IC   Ice crystals

RA   Rain

PL   Ice pellets

SN   Snow

GR   Hail

SG   Snow grains

GS   Small hail/snow pellets

UP   Unknown (in automatic observations)

Obscuration

BR   Mist (visibility > 5/8SM)

FG Fog (visibility 5/8SM or less)

SA Sand

FU Smoke

HZ Haze

VA Volcanic Ash

PY Spray

DU Dust

Other

SQ Squall

FC Funnel Cloud

SS Sandstorm

+FC Tornado/Waterspout, well developed funnel cloud

DS Dust storm

PO Well developed dust/sand whirls

BKN015 OVC025

SKY CONDITION

Cloud amount and height:

CLR (no clouds below 12000 feet, automated reports only)

SKC Sky clear, 0/8

FEW Few, 1/8-2/8

SCT Scattered, 3/8-4/8

BKN Broken, 5/8-7/8

OVC Overcast, 8/8

3-digit height of base in hundreds of feet; followed by cloud type is Towering Cumulus (TCU) or Cumulonimbus (CB) if present. For an observed sky: Vertical Visibility followed by vertical visibility in hundreds of feet into the obscuration, example: VV004. More than 1 layer may be reported.

09/05

TEMPERATURE/DEW POINT

Each is reported in whole degrees Celsius using two digits; values are separated by a forward slash (/); sub-zero values are prefixed with an M (minus).

A2990

ALTIMETER

Altimeter setting (in US reports) is always prefixed with an A indicating inches of mercury; reported using four digits: tens, units, tenths, and hundredths.

RMK

REMARKS IDENTIFIER

Remarks include clarifying or augmenting data concerning elements in the body of the METAR, additive coded data and maintenance data.

AO2

TYPE OF AUTOMATED STATION

AO1   Automated station without a precipitation discriminator.

AO2   Automated station with precipitation discriminator.

PK WND 31020/28

PEAK WIND

Peak wind, dddff(f)/(hh))mm, given in direction in tens of degrees (ddd), speed in whole knots (ff(f)/time in minutes after the hour(mm). Only

248

minutes after the hour is included if the hour can be inferred from the report

WSHFT 1920

WIND SHIFT

WSHFT followed by hours and minutes of occurrence. The term FROPA may be entered after the time if it is reasonably certain that the wind shift was a result of a frontal passage.

VIS 3/4V1 1/2

PREVAILING VISIBLITY

Reported if visibility is <3SM and variable.

VIS 3/4RWY27

VISIBILTY AT SECOND LOCATION

Reported if different than the reported visibility in the main body of the report.

RAB24

BEGINNING AND ENDING OF PRECIPITATION AND THUNDERSTORMS

Describes when precipitation or thunderstorms began or ended using format: "XX"B(hh)mm or "XX"E(hh)mm. "XX" is the precipitation identifier or "TS" for thunderstorms. B indicates began, E indicates ended. (HH) is the two digit hour, given if it cannot be inferred from the report. mm indicates the minutes after the hour the precipitation began or ended.

CIG 013V017

VARIABLE CEILING

Ceiling, in hundreds of feet, reported if the ceiling in the body of the report is < 3000 feet and variable

CIG 017RWY27

CEILING HEIGHT AT SECOND LOCATION

Ceiling height in hundreds of feet, reported if secondary site ceiling value is different than the ceiling height in the body of the report.

PRESFR

PRESSURE RISING OR FALLING RAPIDLY

PRESRR or PRESFR; pressure rising or falling rapidly at time of observation.

SLP125

SEA LEVEL PRESSURE

SLPppp; sea level pressure reported for ppp in tens, units, and tenths of hPa.

P0004

HOURLY PRECIPITATION AMOUNT

Prrrr; in tens, units, tenths and hundredths of an inch since last regular hourly METAR.

60010

3- AND 6-HOUR PRECIPITATION AMOUNT

6RRRR, 3RRRR; precipitation amount, including water equivalent, to nearest 0.01 inches for past 6 hours reported in 00, 06, 12, and 18 UTC observations and for past 3 hours in 03, 09, 15, and 21 UTC observations. A trace is 60000.

HOURLY TEMPERATURE AND DEW POINT

TXyyyXddd; "yyy" is the temperature and "ddd" is the dew point reported to nearest tenth of a degree Celsius. "X" is 1 if temperature or dew point is below 0 degrees C and 0 if temperature/dew point is 0 degrees C or higher.

10099

6-HOUR MAXIMUM TEMPERATURE

1Xyyy; "yyy" is the maximum temperature for past 6 hours reported to nearest tenth of a degree Celsius; reported on 00, 06, 12, 18 UTC reports; "X" is 1 if temperature below 0 degrees C and 0 if temperature is 0 degrees C or higher.

21014

6-HOUR MINIMUM TEMPERATURE

2Xyyy; "yyy" is the minimum temperature for past 6 hours reported to nearest tenth of a degree Celsius; reported on 00, 06, 12, 18 UTC reports. "X" is 1 if temperature below 0 degrees C and 0 if temperature is 0 degrees C or higher.

58033

PRESSURE TENDENCY

5Appp; "A" is the trend of pressure change and "ppp" is the amount of change in pressure in tenths of hPa for the past 3 hours.

TSNO

SENSOR STATUS INDICATORS

RVRNO	RVR missing
PWINO	Precipitation identifier information not available
PNO	Precipitation amount not available
FZRANO	Freezing rain information not available
TSNO	Thunderstorm information not available
VISNO [LOC]	Visibility at second location not available
CHINO [LOC]	Cloud height indicator at secondary location not available

$

MAINTENANCECHECK INDICATOR

Maintenance is needed on the system

Other remarks, not included on this report:

TORNADO, FUNNEL CLOUD or WATERSPOUT

TORNADIC ACTIVITY

Report should include TORNADO, FUNNEL CLOUD or WATERSPOUT, time (after the hour) of beginning/end, location, movement; e.g., **TORNADO B25 N MOVE E**

TWR VIS 2

TOWER OR SURFACE VISIBILITY

TWR VIS vvvvv: visibility reported by tower personnel

SFC VIS vvvvv: visibility reported by ASOS or observer

LIGHTNING

When detected, lightning is reported as (Frequency) LTG (type) (Location). Frequency is listed as occasional (OCNL), Frequent (FRQ), or Continuous (CONS)

Type is listed as Cloud-Ground (CG), In Cloud (IC), Cloud-Cloud (CC), or Cloud-Air (CA)

VIRGA

VIRGA PRESENT

Indicates precipitation not reaching the ground is observed.

70019

24-HOUR PRECIPITATION AMOUNT

7RRRR; precipitation amount to nearest 0.01 inches for past 24 hours reported in 12 UTC observation.

400991014

24-HOUR MAXIMUM AND MINIMUM TEMPERATURE

4XyyyXzzz; "yyy" is the maximum temperature for past 24 hours reported to nearest tenth of degree Celsius and "zzz" is the minimum temperature for past 24 hours reported to nearest tenth of degree Celsius. "X" is 1 if temperature is below 0 degrees C and 0 if temperature is 0 degrees C or higher.

How long is a TAF valid?

Twenty-four hours, unless the TAF has been corrected or delayed. The valid time is listed in the TAF (see Decoded TAF, below)

Decode a TAF

```
TAF
KDPA 061130Z 061212 14008KT 4SM BR BKN030 TEMPO 1316
1 1/2SM BR
FM1600 18010KT P6SM SKC
BECMG 2224 20013G20KT 4SM SHRA OVC020 PROB40 0006 2SM
TSRA OVC008CB
BECMG 0608 21015KT P6SM NSW SCT040=
```

TAF

TYPE OF REPORT

TAF	Terminal Aerodrome Forecast
TAF AMD	Amended Terminal Aerodrome Forecast

KDPA

ICAO STATION INDENTIFIER

061130Z

DATE AND TIME TAF WAS PREPARED

DDHHmmz format, where DD is the day of the month and HHmm is the time in UTC. This forecast was prepared on the sixth day of the month and 1130zulu. TAFs have four schedule issuance times: 00z, 06z, 12z, and 18z. The reports are usually prepared 30 minutes prior to the scheduled issuance time, however any reports prepared from the hour prior to the fourth hour past the scheduled issuance time are considered part of that observing cycle. For example, any report produced 1100-1659 is considered to be the 12z forecast.

061212

VALID PERIOD DATE AND TIME

DDHHhh format, where DD is the two digit date, HH is the beginning hour, and hh is the ending hour. This forecast is valid from 1200z on the sixth until 1200z on the seventh. Valid periods beginning at 0000z are indicated as 00, while valid periods ending at 0000z are indicated as 24. The valid time may be less than 24 hours, if the forecast is corrected (COR) or delayed (RTD).

14008KT

SURFACE WINDS

DDDsssKT format, where DDD is the wind direction and sss is the speed (only two digits if wind is less than 100knots). KT follows the number to denote knots of wind. Wind gusts are noted by a G followed by the max gust speed in knots, example 20013G20KT. Calm winds (3 knots or less) are shown as 0000KT. If the wind direction cannot be determined, VRB (variable) is used in place of the three digit wind direction.

4SM

VISIBILTY

Prevailing visibility in miles or fractions of miles. If the forecast visibility is greater than 6 statute miles, P6SM will be noted.

BR

WEATHER

Qualifier of Intensity or Proximity

    –   Light

    (no sign)   Moderate

    +   Heavy

    VC   Vicinity (5-10SM) but not at aerodrome

Descriptor

    MI   Shallow

255

BL	Blowing
BC	Patches
SH	Showers
PR	Partial
DR	Drifting
TS	Thunderstorm
FZ	Freezing

Precipitation

DZ	Drizzle
IC	Ice crystals
RA	Rain
PL	Ice pellets
SN	Snow
GR	Hail
SG	Snow grains
GS	Small hail/snow pellets

Obscuration

BR	Mist (visibility > 5/8SM)
FG	Fog (visibility 5/8SM or less)
SA	Sand
FU	Smoke
HZ	Haze
VA	Volcanic Ash
PY	Spray
DU	Dust

Other

SQ	Squall
FC	Funnel Cloud

SS	Sandstorm
+FC	Tornado/Waterspout, well developed funnel cloud
DS	Dust storm
PO	Well developed dust/sand whirls

Obstructions to visibility are reported if prevailing visibility is forecast to be 6 statute miles or less.

If no significant weather is forecast, it will omitted. If significant weather is forecast, but later forecasts have none, NSW (no significant weather) will be noted.

BKN030

SKY CONDITION

Same format as METAR, except cumulonimbus (CB) are the only cloud types in a TAF.

Cloud amount and height:

CLR (no clouds below 12000 feet, automated reports only)

SKC	Sky Clear, 0/8
FEW	Few, 1/8-2/8
SCT	Scattered, 3/8-4/8
BKN	Broken, 5/8-7/8
OVC	Overcast, 8/8

3-digit height of base in hundreds of feet. For an observed sky, vertical visibility is reported in hundreds of feet into the obscuration, example:

VV004 is vertical visibility 400 feet.

TEMPO 1316 1 1/2SM BR

TEMPORARY GROUP

Used if a changing condition of wind, visibility, weather, or sky condition is expected to last for less than an hour at a time, and occur for less than half the time period. The numbers following TEMPO represent the beginning and ending hours for which the condition is expected. Only the conditions that change from the primary forecast are included in the temporary forecast. In this example, from 1300z to 1600z, occasional periods of visibility down to one and a half statute miles are forecast due to mist.

FM1600 18010KT P6SM SKC

FROM GROUP

Used when a rapid change in the prevailing weather is expected. FMtttt format, where tttt is the four digit time the change will begin. The weather is valid from that time until the next change, or the end of the forecast. A from group will contain the wind, visibility, weather, and sky condition.

BECMG 2224 20013G20KT 4SM SHRA OVC020

BECOMING GROUP

Used when a gradual change is expected over a longer period of time (usually 2 hours). BECMMG TTtt, format, where TT is the hours the gradual change is expected to begin and tt is the time the change is expected to be complete. Only the conditions that are expected to change are included.

PROB40 0006 2SM TSRA OVC008CB

PROBABILITY FORECAST

Used when there is a probability, or chance, of thunderstorms or other precipitation events occurring. PROBpp TTtt format where pp is the percentage chance that this event will occur, TT is the hour the probability begins, and tt is the hour the probability no longer applies. The event and its associated weather will be shown.

=

END

Marks the end of an individual TAF, usually used if several TAFs are bundled together and sent as one transmission.

Other remarks, not included on this report:

NIL AMD SKED AFT 0500z

NO FORECAST UPDATES DUE TO FACILITY CLOSURE

Part time airports or terminals will include this note to show no updates are available. TAFs issued during the closure will have NIL in place of text. After the facility opens again, a delayed (RTD) forecast will be issued.

WS010/18040KT

WINDSHEAR

WShhh/DDDsss format for reporting non-convective low level winds (up to 2000 feet), where "WS" denotes wind shear followed by height (hhh) in hundreds of feet AGL, DDD is wind direction and sss is wind speed in the same format as surface winds.

Decode a Winds Aloft Forecast

```
DATA BASED ON 030000Z
VALID 010600Z     FOR USE 0500-0900Z.  TEMPS NEG ABV
24000
FT   3000      6000      9000     12000     18000     24000
30000  34000   39000
MKC  2426  2726-09  2826-14  2930-21  2744-32  2751-41
770550 771250 750647
```

DDTTTT that the computer generated this forecast. In this example, the forecast was generated on the 3rd day of the month at 0000z.

VALID 030600Z   FOR USE 0500-0900Z. TEMPS NEG ABV 24000

The valid time of the forecast is 0600z on the 3rd day of the month
The forecast winds and temperatures should be used between 0500z and 0900z
Temperatures are negative above 24,000.

FT   3000   6000   9000   12000   18000   24000
30000   34000   39000

Below FT is the forecast location.
Numbers are the altitudes.
All altitudes through 12,000 ft are MSL.
All altitudes of 18,000 ft and above are pressure altitude.

MKC   2426   2726-09   2826-14   *2930-21*   2744-32   2751-41
770550 *771250* 750647

Wind direction is from true north.

Winds are rounded to the nearest 10 degree increment.

No winds are forecast within 1,500 ft of station elevation.

Temperatures are in whole degrees Celsius.

No temps are forecast at the 3,000 ft level, or within 2500 ft of station elevation.

If the wind is less than 5 knots, the report will show 9900.

MKC is the station, in this case Kansas City, MO.

Format: DDSS(+/-)TT, example one: 2930-21, example two: 771250

DD is wind direction from true north rounded to the nearest ten degrees.

Example one, the wind direction is 290 degrees. If the wind speed is 100 kts or greater, the 100 is subtracted from the wind speed, and fifty is added to the wind direction. Example two, the wind direction is 270 (77-50=27).

SS is wind speed in knots. Example one, the wind speed is 30 knots. If the wind speed is 100 kts or greater, the 100 is subtracted from the wind speed, and fifty is added to the wind direction. Example two, the wind speed is 112 knots (12+100).

TT is temperature in Celsius. Example one, the temperature is -21 degrees Celsius. The (+/-) is omitted above 24,000 ft as all temperatures above are negative. Example two, the temperature is -50 degrees Celsius.

What is the primary cause of weather?

Unequal heating of the earth's surface.

What are the types of ice?

- Rime Ice- forms when the temperature is -15°C or colder. Small drops freeze quickly at cold temperatures so there is little flow back and the ice forms on the leading edge. In-flight anti-ice systems tend to be on the leading edges so they are typically effective against rime ice.
- Clear Ice- forms when the temperature is -10°C or warmer. Larger drops hit the leading edge and spread out on the wing surfaces (flow back) before freezing. Clear ice will often form further back than the anti-ice systems can protect, so this is the most dangerous type of in-flight icing.
- Mixed Ice- forms when temperatures are between -10°C and -15°C. This is a mix of droplet sizes and a combination of rime and clear ice.

What are the different types of de-ice/anti-ice fluids?

- Type I: De-icing only. This glycol/water mix is orange in color and applied hot to clean the surfaces.
- Type II- De-icing/Anti-icing: Applied cold as an anti-ice agent or applied warm to de-ice as well. This pale straw, or water white, colored fluid has thickening agents added which allow it to adhere to the wing. Precipitation will sit on top of the fluid until the fluid shears from the wing (taking the precipitation with it) on the takeoff roll.
- Type IV- Anti-icing: Type IV fluid is similar to type II, but can resist colder temperatures and more exposure to freezing precipitation. This green colored fluid has thickening agents added which allow it to adhere to the wing. Precipitation will sit on top of the fluid until the fluid shears from the wing (taking the precipitation with it) on the takeoff roll.

What is a holdover time?

Holdover time is the estimated time that a de-ice/anti-ice fluid can prevent formation of frozen precipitation on the airplane. It is only a guide to help the awareness of the pilot and does not represent a mandatory time.

What is a pre-takeoff check?

A pre-takeoff check is a check of the aircraft's wings or representative aircraft surfaces for frost, ice, or snow within the aircraft's holdover time.

What is a pre-takeoff contamination check?

A visual check of the wings, required by most airlines, to ensure the wings are free of freezing precipitation. This check must be accomplished if any precipitation has fallen after the de-ice/anti-ice fluid was applied and must be completed no more than 5 minutes prior to takeoff.

What causes ice pellets and/or freezing rain?

Ice pellets are caused by rain in warm air above falling through a cold section of air. If the band of cold air is narrow, the rain will become freezing rain, and not become solid until striking the cold surface of the aircraft. If the band of cold air is thicker than a few hundred feet, the rain will freeze into ice pellets.

What are the worst conditions for icing?

Heavy freezing drizzle has the flow back characteristics of freezing rain, but it also has very high liquid water concentration, which leads to large and oddly shaped ice deposits on the wing. Ridges of ice can form along the entire wingspan and drastically reduce lift.

How much ice can you legally take off with?

None.

91.157

Definition of severe icing.

The rate of accumulation on an aircraft is such that de-icing/anti-icing equipment fails to reduce or control the hazard and an immediate diversion is necessary.

What type of ice would you expect in a cumulous cloud?

Clear ice, due to the presence of large water droplets.

Convert RVR to SM

- RVR 1600   ¼ SM
- RVR 2400   ½ SM
- RVR 4000   ¾ SM
- RVR 5000   1 SM

What weather is required for takeoff?

- Standard takeoff minimums:
  - 1 mile (5000 RVR) for two engine aircraft
  - ½ mile (2400 RVR) for aircraft with three or more engines

When the weather is 800/2, do you have to stop short of an ILS critical area marker?

Not unless ATC advised to do so.

What is a SMGCS chart?

Low visibility taxi charts.   SMGCS stands for Surface Movement Guidance Control System.

When are SMGCS procedures in effect?

Special labels in the heading will indicate specific usage. For example, SMGCS procedures will be in effect when visibility is less than 1200 RVR, as listed on the chart.

Definition of tropopause.

The tropopause is the boundary between the troposphere and the stratosphere. It is the point at which the temperature stops decreasing with altitude and the point under which all weather occurs.

How does the jet stream affect flight decisions?

When the winds are strong, the jet stream can play an important role in determining optimum altitudes. Changing cruise altitude to get a strong tailwind can offset the decrease in engine efficiency by increasing the groundspeed and thereby increasing the range. Conversely, a strong headwind should be avoided because of its negative effects on cruise performance. The jet stream should also be considered for possible clear air turbulence, which is strongest on the polar side next to or just below the axis of the jet.

What can weather radar tell you?

Precipitation intensity.

What is weather radar attenuation and what can you do about it?

Weather radar sends out a signal that reflects off precipitation and returns back to the radar receiver. In most cases, the radar beam continues through the precipitation to interpret what is behind. If the band of precipitation is too heavy, it will block the beam from continuing past and looking behind. This is radar attenuation. On the screen, this will appear as a band of weather with no returns behind it, making it tempting to go that way.

What type a precipitation shows up best on radar?
Wet hail.

What are the types of fog?
- Radiation fog- On calm, clear nights, the earth cools (radiational cooling), causing the air on the surface to cool as well. If the air cools to less than the dew point, fog forms.
- Advection fog- With light winds, warm humid air flows over cooler ground or water.
- Precipitation fog- Precipitation falling though cold air will add more moisture to the air than it is able to hold.
- Upslope fog- Humid air being pushed up rising terrain will cool. If cooled to the dew point, fog forms.
- Steam fog- Cold air moving over warm water will acquire enough water to form fog.
- Ice fog- At very cold temperatures, the tiny particles of water that form fog at normal temperatures will freeze and become suspended particles of ice.

Temp/dew point spread was 19/19. What weather could you expect?
Fog.

Describe a cold front.
- Bubble of cold air moving across the surface forcing warmer air over it causing:
  - Unstable air
  - Turbulence
  - Good visibility
  - Showery precipitation

Describe a warm front.

- Upward sloping wedge of warm air forcing cooler air under it causing:
    o Stable air
    o Smooth air
    o Poor visibility
    o Steady precipitation

Weather associated with a low pressure system?

- Strong winds
- Atmospheric lift
- Overcast skies
- Bad weather

Weather associated with a high pressure system?

- Stable air
- Clear skies
- Calm winds

What is required for a thunderstorm to form?

- Air with high moisture content
- Lifting action
- Unstable lapse rate

What are the stages of a thunderstorm?

- Cumulus Stage- Defined by updrafts, exceeding 3000 feet per minute, and the beginning of visible moisture within the cloud.
- Mature Stage- Defined by precipitation beginning to fall from the cloud. As precipitation falls, it cools the air and accelerates the downward movement creating gusting winds, high pressure and decreasing temperatures at the surface. Updrafts can reach 6000 feet per minute and downdrafts may exceed 2500 feet per minute within a close proximity, creating strong vertical sheer and severe turbulence within the cloud.
- Dissipating Stage- Downdrafts characterize the dissipating stage. When the rain ends, and the downdrafts have stopped, the life cycle of the thunderstorm is complete.

What weather can you expect when updrafts go into the stratosphere?

Severe thunderstorms.

What are the differences between air mass and steady state thunderstorms?

- Air mass thunderstorms are usually created by surface heating. As the mature stage begins, the rain falls through the updrafts causing them to slow and turn to downdrafts, making this type of thunderstorm self-destructive. These normally form over the land in the late afternoon when the surface is hottest.
- Steady state thunderstorms are typically associated with a weather system. Fronts and converging winds at the surface along with troughs aloft create the lifting action. These thunderstorms are often seen in squall lines, and will intensify with afternoon surface heating. Precipitation often falls outside of the updrafts as these storms form on a slant. The mature stage will not dissipate the storm, so these last much longer, and become stronger than air mass storms.

What is a squall line?

A squall line is a non-frontal, narrow band of active thunderstorms. Squall lines often develop ahead of a cold front in moist, unstable air, but it can develop in unstable air far removed from any front. The lines usually form rapidly, may be too long to easily detour, and too wide and severe to penetrate. Squall lines often contain severe steady-state thunderstorms and may produce tornadoes. Maximum intensity is reached in the late afternoon.

Here is a thunderstorm, and here is the anvil. Which way is it moving? What weather can we expect under the anvil?

The anvil points downwind. You can expect turbulence and hail.

What is the definition of a severe thunderstorm?

- Surface gusts of 50 kts or greater
- Surface hail of ¾ inch or more in diameter
- Tornadoes

How far away should you be, avoiding a thunderstorm?

Twenty miles laterally, preferably upwind. Clear the top by 1000 ft for every 10 knots of wind at altitude.

What do you do if you inadvertently fly into a thunderstorm?

- Tighten your seat belt
- Plan the shortest route straight ahead to exit the storm, and don't turn from it
- Turn on all airplane heating elements
- Maintain power setting for turbulence penetration speed
- Turn cockpit lights to full bright (reduces lightning effects)
- Maintain pitch attitude; don't chase altitude

What is a microburst?

A microburst is a localized intense downdraft, which spreads out in a circular pattern where it strikes the surface. A microburst is extremely hazardous to all types of aircraft and can cause both vertical and horizontal wind shears.

What would you do if you encountered wind shear on approach to landing?

Go around. Do not change the configuration of the aircraft until you are clear of the wind shear.

What initial cockpit indications should a pilot be aware of when a head wind shears to a calm wind?

- Indicated airspeed decreases
- Aircraft pitches down
- Altitude decreases

What initial cockpit indications should a pilot be aware of when a calm wind shears to a head wind?

- Indicated airspeed increases
- Aircraft pitches up
- Altitude increases

What is a mountain wave?

Stable air flowing over a mountain causes oscillation of the air on the leeward side. These oscillations can influence air 100 miles downwind of the mountain and are associated with turbulence.

What is the lowest cloud in the stationary group associated with a mountain wave?

Rotor cloud.

Where is the most turbulence in relation to a rotor cloud?

In and below the cloud.

Which types of clouds are indicative of very strong turbulence?

Standing lenticular, which form at the crest of mountain waves.

When will your altimeter read higher than you actually are?

In very cold air.

When will frost form on the wings?

Frost forms when the temperature of the wing is at or below the dew point of the surrounding air and the dew point is below freezing.

What is St. Elmo's fire?

St. Elmo's fire is an electrical weather phenomenon in which luminous plasma is created by a coronal (electrical build-up) discharge. This is seen in the cockpit as what looks like small lighting flashes on the windscreens, and it is perfectly safe.

What flight conditions are associated with a temperature inversion?
- Smooth, stable air
- Temperature increase with altitude
- Poor visibility due to trapped pollutants, fog, haze, or low clouds

What is the average height of the tropopause?

Thirty-six thousand feet.

What is maximum height of the tropopause?

Sixty thousand feet.

What is the standard temperature lapse rate?

Temperature decreases 2 degrees Celsius per each 1000 ft of elevation.

If weather in TEMPO is bad, do you need an alternate?

Yes.

Definition of ISA, temp and pressure?

At sea level ISA is 15 degrees Celsius and altimeter 29.92 inches of mercury (hg).

What is an isobar?

Line of equal pressure on a weather map.

What type of weather is reported in an ARIMET?

Moderate icing, moderate turbulence, sustained winds of 30 knots or more at surface, IFR conditions, or extensive mountain obscuration.

What type of weather is reported in a SIGMET?

- Widespread (3,000sq miles or greater) severe icing or turbulence not associated with a thunderstorm
- Dust storms or sandstorms lowering the visibility to less than 3 miles
- Volcanic ash

What is reported in a convective SIGMET?

- Tornadoes
- Line of thunderstorms
- Thunderstorms over a wide area (40 percent of a 3,000sq mile area)
- Embedded thunderstorms
- Hail ¾ inch or greater in diameter
- Thunderstorms with wind gusts of 50 knots or greater

What is the best report for finding convective activity along a route?

PIREP.

What are QNH, QFE, QNE?

- These are different heights as read off the altimeter
    - QNH: Height above sea level (local altimeter setting)
    - QFE: Height above field elevation (Field Elevation)
    - QNE: Height above 29.92 (standard altimeter setting)

What are the Santa Ana winds?

These winds start as high pressure air on the tops of the Sierra Nevada and Rocky Mountains and travels down slopes toward the oceans of California. As the already dry, cool air descends, it warms and adiabatically dries which increases the rate of descent. Also adding to the wind speed is the funneling effect of the valleys and canyons. These winds can reach hurricane force and are most common in the autumn and early spring.

What are the Chinook winds?

Chinook winds are known for drastic increases in temperature and are mostly found in the northern US and southern Canadian Rocky Mountains. When wet pacific air is forced up the side of the Rocky Mountains, it cools at the wet adiabatic lapse rate until reaching the point of saturation, then releases its moisture in the form of rain or snow. The now dry parcel of air reaches the top of the mountain and starts down on the leeward side, increasing temperature at the dry adiabatic lapse rate. Because the dry adiabatic lapse rate is greater than the wet adiabatic lapse rate, the air has gained much more temperature in the descent than it lost in the ascent. The result is a large temperature increase on the eastern side of the mountain, often associated with sudden snow melts.

Chart Knowledge

Definitions

MAA- Maximum Authorized Altitude; the highest usable altitude allowed on an airway or jet route. This restriction assures navigation coverage along the route. *On the chart-* listed as "MAA" followed by the maximum flight level (MAA FL370).

MCA- Minimum Crossing Altitude; lowest altitude at which an airplane must cross certain fixes when proceeding in the direction of a higher MEA. *On the chart-* listed as "MCA" followed by flight level, or altitude, and the flight direction of the aircraft for which the crossing restriction applies (MCA FL190 NW).

MEA- Minimum En Route Altitude; lowest altitude between radio fixes that assures terrain clearance and navigation aid coverage. *On the chart-* listed as the flight level or altitude (4200), direction MEAs are followed by an arrow denoting flight direction; only listed on high charts if MEA is higher than flight level 180, on some charts a "G" may follow the MEA number to identify the MEA for the route if GPS is being used for navigation (9200G).

MIA- Minimum IFR Altitude; lowest altitude for IFR operation, defined in designated mountainous areas as 2,000 ft above the highest obstacle within 4 NM of course flown, or in other than mountainous areas, 1,000 ft above the highest obstacle within 4 NM of course flown. *On the chart-* not listed.

MOCA- Minimum Obstruction Clearance Altitude; lowest altitude between radio fixes on VOR airways which assure obstacle clearance along the entire route and navigational coverage within 22 NM of a VOR. *On the chart*- listed as the altitude followed by a "T" (2300T).

MORA- Minimum Off-Route Altitude; lowest altitude required for terrain separation when not on a federally defined route. Clears all terrain by 1000 ft in areas where the highest elevation is 5000 ft MSL or lower; and 2000 ft in areas where the highest terrain is 5001 ft MSL or higher. When marked inside the lat/long sections of the chart, this is called a "grid MORA." When listed for a route that is not federally defined, this is called a "route MORA." *On the chart*- a route MORA is listed as altitude or flight level followed by an "a" (3600a). A grid MORA is a large bold number listed in thousands and hundreds of feet and are green numbers when less than 14,000 ft, and magenta when 14,000 ft or higher (155). Grid MORA values followed by a + / - denote doubtful accuracy, but are believed to provide sufficient reference point clearance.

MSA- Minimum Safe Altitude or Minimum Sector Altitude; on an approach plate, the lowest altitude within 25 NM of the navigational aid upon which the approach is based that provides 1,000 ft of terrain clearance from the highest obstacle. If the 25 NM is centered on another navigation aid, it will be listed under the circle. The circle may be divided into sectors of at least 90 degrees in scope, in which case MSA stands for minimum sector altitude and provides the same terrain clearance within that sector of the circle. *On the approach chart*- depicted as a circle, representing the 25-mile ring with the altitude(s) listed inside; sectors will be defined by magnetic courses, "MSA." The navigational aid will be written under the circle.

MVA- Minimum Vectoring Altitude; lowest altitude at which an IFR aircraft will be vectored by ATC. *On the chart*- only listed on controller charts, not available to pilots.

TDZE– Touchdown Zone Elevation; highest point in the first 3,000 ft of the landing runway.

En Route, Area Charts

How do you tell the difference between a high altitude en route chart and a low altitude en route chart?
- Upper corners of the chart will show "(HI)" or "(LO)"
- Victor airways (low) instead of jet routes (high)
- Rivers and lakes depicted on low chart, only very large bodies of water on a high chart
- Airspace is identified on low altitude charts (class B, C, D, E)

How high are victor airways?
From 1200 ft up to, but not including 18,000 ft.

How high are jet routes?
From 18,000 ft MSL up to and including flight level 450.

How wide are victor airways?
Four NM either side of the route; 8 miles total.

What does a flag over a navaid mean?
Magnetic north ticks for use with plotters.

How do you know if this area on the chart contains mountainous terrain?

Referencing the mountainous terrain designation map from 14 CFR 95 to determine if the area is officially considered mountainous (see AIM chapter). For situational awareness when looking at the chart, any MORA over 7000 ft indicates the highest terrain in that region is greater than 5000 ft.

Why does one DME distance have a D with an arrow and the other has a D, arrow, and number?

A "D" with an arrow and number indicates total DME distance from a navaid. On the first segment from a navaid, when the segment length and the total distance are the same, the number following the "D" is omitted.

When changing course on an airway, are you expected to lead your turn?

Yes, unless the point is a flyover point, which is depicted by a circle around the fix.

What must you consider when going direct between navaids?

- Obstruction clearance
- Navaid signal coverage

Where is the changeover point on an airway?

- At a defined fix, depicted as a triangle on the chart
- At a mileage break/turning point that is not a defined fix, depicted as an "X"
- At the changeover point symbol, which looks like a step across the airway, with numbers representing the distance to each navaid

Difference between blue and green airports.

- Blue airports have an IFR published procedure
- Green airports are VFR airports

What do the numbers after the airport identifier represent?

- Airport elevation and longest runway to the nearest 100 ft rounded up (71 equals 7100 ft).
- "s" indicates a soft runway surface

Military vs. civilian airports

- Military airports are smooth circles
- Civilian airports are circles with notched edges

VOR information

- Shadow box = part of the route
- "D" = DME capability
- (H), (L), (T) = VOR service volume designation
- Lat/Long depicted= VOR is part of the high altitude route structure
- Frequency above the navaid= voice available through the navaid using the radio frequency shown. If listed with a "G," the facility can hear (guard) the radio frequency but transmits over the VOR frequency
- Telephone symbol = more radio frequencies are available somewhere else on the chart
- HIWAS = hazardous weather info broadcasts over the VOR continuously
- "WX" = flight watch available through station shown
- "*" next to frequency = not continuous

Why are some fixes solid?

A solid fix is a compulsory reporting point.

What does a circled "M" indicate?

Meteorological reporting point. Give temperature, wind, icing, turbulence, clouds and any significant weather to the station indicated.

How do you find where an MEA changes?

MEA change occurs when the line representing the route has a line perpendicular to it prior to a fix or navaid. The route line after the fix or navaid will also have a perpendicular line representing the starting point for the new MEA. These lines also indicate changes to a MOCA or MORA if no MEA is listed.

How can you tell if navigation coverage is not continuous along a route?

An MEA gap symbol will be shown as a solid rectangle with a jagged break through it.

Why do some airways make a half circle around some fixes?

The fix is not a part of that route.

What is the brown line of "MWMWMWMWMW"?

Mountain wave region.

Based on an en-route chart, on what frequency would you contact center?

A line of alternating upside down and right side up telephones denotes radio frequency sector boundaries. Use frequency found inside a box with agency name within this boundary. If no telephone symbol, a thin black line with alternating tick marks highlighted green shows the ARTCC facility boundary and all available frequencies for each ARTCC facility can be found on the front page of the chart.

What does the gray shaded part of the low chart represent?

Uncontrolled airspace.

When are terrain contours shown on area charts?

When terrain within the chart rises more than 4000 ft above the primary airport.

How are arrival routes different from departure routes on an area chart?

Arrival routes are dashed lines with an arrow at the end, while departure routes are solid lines with an arrow at the end. If an arrival and departure are on the same route, the line is solid with no arrow.

Describe the different tracks on a SID/STAR.

- Transition track is a dashed line followed by an arrow
- SID/STAR track is a solid line followed by an arrow
- Radar vectors are displayed as a series of small arrow heads touching each other
- Visual flight track is a series of spaced medium arrows in a row

Approach Charts

Give an approach briefing.

- Don't read the entire chart. Any order is fine as long as the items below are included. Using the chart can help to organize your brief- read the heading, briefing strip, visibility required, and MSA.
- Briefing items to include:
    - Approach chart number and date
    - Approach name
    - Navaid
    - Inbound course
    - FAF crossing altitude
    - Minimums
    - Time or distance to MAP (if non-precision)
    - Missed approach procedure
    - Visibility required starting the approach
    - MSA
- Other items that may be included if they are of concern to safety
    - ATIS/NOTAMs
    - Airplane/MEL restrictions
    - Wind shear/weather
    - Runway condition
    - Approach speed
    - Runway exit plan
    - Taxi considerations/hotspots

Where is the highest point on the chart?

The highest point is referenced by a think black arrow on the plan view.

What is the difference between thick lines with large arrowheads and thin lines with small arrowheads on the plan view?

Thick lines with large arrowheads are approach transitions that can be flown. Thin lines with small arrowheads denote radials that define fixes on the approach.

Explain the altitudes on the plan view.

- All altitudes are minimums unless labeled otherwise
- MANDATORY means the altitude must be flown if cleared for the approach
- MAXIMUM or MAX means highest allowed if cleared for the approach
- RECOMMENDED altitudes are not required
- Altitudes surrounded by parentheses "()" are AGL

What kind a course reversal should be flown?

When course reversal is required, it must be flown as charted.

Altitudes Used

- Decision Altitude (DA)   MSL
- Decision Height (DH)   AGL
- Minimum Descent Altitude (MDA) MSL

What is the Maltese cross symbol on the approach plate?

Final approach fix for a non-precision approach.

What is "M" on the approach plate?

Missed approach point for non-precision approach.

What is "V" on the approach plate?

Visual descent point.

When do straight in minimums apply?

The approach is within 30° of runway centerline, and

you can descend from the minimum altitude and land in the touchdown zone using normal maneuvers.

How would you estimate distances on the plan view?

The left side of the chart has tick marks with a scale (typically 1 in = 5 NM) for determining distances on the plan view.

Airport Diagram

Discuss taxiing to a runway using the airport diagram

- Frequencies to use
- Routing (Ramp, Ground Metering, Ground)
- Holding short of all runways
- Hotspots

What are the red circles on airport diagrams?

Hotspots- places where runway incursions are the highest possibility and taxi confusion is possible.

What does the asterisk (*) next to the tower in the communications section indicate?

Part-time operation.

Where is the airport beacon?

It is identified by a star with a circle around it.

What is the D stand for in D-ATIS?

Digital.

What does ARP look like and mean on the airport diagram?

The ARP, airport reference point, is a plus with a circle around it (similar to a cross hair) or an arrow pointing to it if the ARP is located on a runway. The ARP is the point upon which the lat/long coordinates of the airport are based.

Where can you find the takeoff minimums?

Back of the airport diagram page.

How is adequate visual reference defined as it pertains to take-off minimums box?

- At least one of the following must apply:
    - Operative high intensity runway lights (HIRL)
    - Operative runway centerline lights (CL)
    - Runway centerline markings (RCLM)
    - When none of those are available; other runway markings and/or lights provide pilots with the adequate visual reference to continuously identify the take-off surface and maintain directional control throughout the take-off run.

Subjective Questions

Personal

- Tell me about your career up to this point.
- What are your three best traits?
- What is your greatest weakness?
- What is your leadership style?
- What's your definition of professionalism?
- How would you handle working with someone you didn't like?
- Have you ever called in sick?
- How can we be sure these times in your logbook are accurate?
- How do you manage fatigue while flying?
- Tell me about a time you failed to achieve a goal or objective.
- Have you ever failed a check ride? Why?
- How would your co-workers describe you?
- Why do you want to work for this company?
- What can you tell me about this company?
- Have you interviewed anywhere else?
- If you receive multiple job offers, which company is your first choice? Why?
- Why did you leave your previous employer?
- What didn't you like about a previous employer?
- How would you handle flying with a crewmember who didn't follow the rules?
- Have you ever bent or broken an FAR?
- Have you ever witnessed someone break an SOP (standard operating procedure)? What did you do?
- Have you ever seen CRM (crew resource management) break down in the cockpit?
- What makes a good captain?

- What makes a good first officer?
- Why should we hire you over another applicant?

Tell Me About A Time

- Tell me about a time you made a mistake.
- Tell me about an emergency you've had. Would you do anything differently?
- Tell me about a time you bent or broke a procedure.
- Tell me about a time you solved a problem.
- Tell me about a time you did more than what was required.
- Tell me about a time you had a conflict in the cockpit.
- Tell me about a time you were stressed in the cockpit.
- Tell me about a rule or policy you changed.
- Tell me about a time you had to make a quick decision.
- Tell me about a time you made an unpopular decision.

What Would You Do

- What would you do if you smelled alcohol on your captain's breath?
- What would you do if a flight attendant called in flight and said a passenger was acting suspiciously?
- What would you do if a passenger had a medical emergency?
- What would you do if you told a captain to go around but he or she wanted to continue?
- What would you do if a captain wanted you to "bend" an FAR or procedure?

- What would you do if you told the captain a navigation light was burned out, but he or she didn't want to write it up?
- Moderate turbulence is reported ahead. You want to go around the area, but the captain wants to go through it. What would you do?
- You show up for your flight and the captain tells you he's going through a bad divorce, and is behaving strangely. What would you do?

About the author

Rick Hogan has been helping pilots land jobs for over a decade. In that time he has worked to land his own jobs, interviewing successfully at regional airlines, legacy carriers, international airlines, ACMI and package delivery companies. He has been based in the Unites States, the United Kingdom, and Hong Kong. Rick holds FAA and HKCAD (Hong Kong Civil Aviation Department) Airline Transport Pilot Certificates and is type rated on the ATR-42, ATR-72, B747-400, B757, B767, CL-65, and the MD-11. Rick currently resides in Anchorage, AK where his is an instructor pilot on the MD-11.

Made in the USA
San Bernardino, CA
16 September 2016